EASTERN EUROPE AND
THE SOVIET UNION
IN THE WORLD ECONOMY

EASTERN EUROPE AND THE SOVIET UNION IN THE WORLD ECONOMY

Susan M. Collins and Dani Rodrik

INSTITUTE FOR INTERNATIONAL ECONOMICS
WASHINGTON, DC
May 1991

Susan M. Collins, Visiting Fellow at the Institute for International Economics, is Associate Professor of Economics at Harvard University and a Faculty Research Fellow of the National Bureau of Economic Research. She was Senior Staff Economist for the Council of Economic Advisers (1989-90), where analysis of developments in Eastern Europe and the Soviet Union was a major focus of her work.

Dani Rodrik, Visiting Fellow at the Institute for International Economics, is an Associate Professor of Public Policy at Harvard's John F. Kennedy School of Government. He is also a Faculty Research Fellow of the National Bureau of Economic Research and a research fellow of the Centre for Economic Policy Research (London). He has been a consultant to international organizations and several governments, and his publications cover issues in trade theory and policy, exchange rate policy, and economic development.

INSTITUTE FOR INTERNATIONAL ECONOMICS
11 Dupont Circle, NW
Washington, DC 20036
(202) 328-9000   Telex: 261271 IIE UR   FAX: (202) 328-5432

C. Fred Bergsten, *Director*
Linda Griffin Kean, *Director of Publications*

The Institute for International Economics was created by, and receives substantial support from, the German Marshall Fund of the United States.

Printed in the United States of America   93 92 91   3 2 1

Library of Congress Cataloging-in-Publication Data

Collins, Susan Margaret
        Eastern Europe and the Soviet Union in the world economy / Susan M.
        Collins and Dani Rodrik.
        p. cm.—(Policy analyses in international economics: 32)
        Includes bibliographical references.
        ISBN 0-88132-157-5: $12.95
        1. Europe, Eastern—Economic conditions—1989–   . 2. Soviet
Union—Economic conditions—1986–   3. Europe, Eastern—Foreign
economic relations.   4. Soviet Union—Foreign economic relations. 5. Economic history—1971–   6. International economic relations. I. Rodrik,
Dani II. Title. III. Series.
HC244.C5757   1991
337.47—dc20   91-15968
                                                                CIP

Contents

FIGURES

Acknowledgments

Dani Rodrik's work was undertaken while he held an NBER Olin Fellowship. We thank the Institute for International Economics, and Thomas Bayard in particular, for assistance in preparing this study. Comments from C. Fred Bergsten, Richard Cooper, Ishac Diwan, Stanley Fischer, Alan Gelb, Joshua Greene, Catherine Mann, Warwick McKibbin, Richard Portes, David Richardson, Edwin Truman, John Whalley, and John Williamson have led to improvements. Michael Treadway did a superb job of editing the manuscript. Robin Ely helped us in designing our survey. We also thank Amy Liang for background work and Martha Synnott for help in typing. Lisa Robinson provided excellent research assistance.

x

Preface

The peaceful revolutions in Eastern Europe (including the Soviet Union) are among the most dramatic events of the current epoch. A central element of the revolutions in most of these countries is a total reversal of economic policy from central planning to a market orientation. With this study, and our simultaneous release of *The Economic Opening of Eastern Europe* by John Williamson, the Institute is launching a series of analyses of key aspects of these historic transformations.

Previous Institute studies, including my own *America in the World Economy: A Strategy for the 1990s* and *Japan in the World Economy* by Bela Balassa and Marcus Noland, have assessed the impact on the world economy of key countries or regions. We have also addressed the interactions with global economic patterns of Africa, the newly industrializing countries of East Asia, and Latin America. This volume addresses the potential impact on the world economy of the emergence of Eastern Europe and the Soviet Union.

The new study assesses the likely effects of the emerging market economies on world trade and capital flows, and through them on such key variables as interest rates and growth in developing countries. Implications are derived for the United States, Germany, the European Community as a whole, Japan, and different sets of developing nations. Some of the projections are necessarily speculative, but they provide both a framework for analysis and specific estimates that should prove helpful in understanding one of the most important, but heretofore least analyzed, aspects of the Eastern European revolutions.

The Institute for International Economics is a private nonprofit institution for the study and discussion of international economic policy. Its purpose is to analyze important issues in that area, and to develop and communicate practical new approaches for dealing with them. The Institute is completely nonpartisan.

The Institute was created by a generous commitment of funds from the German Marshall Fund of the United States in 1981 and now receives about 12 percent of its support from that source. In addition, major institutional grants are now being received from the Ford Foundation, the William and Flora Hewlett Foundation, the William M. Keck, Jr. Foundation, the Alfred P. Sloan Foundation, the C. V. Starr Foundation, and the United States–Japan Foundation. A number of other foundations and private corporations are contributing to the highly diversified financial resources of the Institute. About 15 percent of those resources in our latest fiscal year were provided by contributors outside the United States, including about 5 percent from Japan.

The Board of Directors bears overall responsibility for the Institute and gives general guidance and approval to its research program— including identification of topics that are likely to become important to international economic policymakers over the medium run (generally, one to three years), and which thus should be addressed by the Institute. The Director, working closely with the staff and outside Advisory Committee, is responsible for the development of particular projects and makes the final decision to publish an individual study.

The Institute hopes that its studies and other activities will contribute to building a stronger foundation for international economic policy around the world. We invite readers of these publications to let us know how they think we can best accomplish this objective.

C. FRED BERGSTEN
Director
May 1991

xii

EASTERN EUROPE AND
THE SOVIET UNION
IN THE WORLD ECONOMY

1 Introduction, Overview, and a Road Map

Social scientists, historians, and political observers in general agree on one point about the Eastern European revolutions of 1989: no one foresaw them. The collapse of Communist power in Eastern Europe, the fall of the Berlin Wall and the reunification of Germany, the implosions in the Soviet Union—the end of the cold war, in short—all these developments unfolded in a remarkably short time and as a huge surprise to "experts" and ordinary television viewers alike. But the lesson—that the utmost modesty is in order when it comes to pronouncements about the future of human societies—does not seem to have sunk in. As soon as those astounding changes in the world's political and economic map took place, numerous voices were heard uttering self-assured opinions about the implications of those changes for this or that country or group of countries. It does not seem to have occurred to these people that if the events, which are the point of departure for their speculations, were so hard to predict, considerable caution is surely in order when it comes to appraising their impact.

Albert O. Hirschman (1990, 20)

This is a study on the economic implications of the integration of Eastern Europe and the Soviet Union into the world economy. For the world economy as whole, the opening of these economies is good news. It promises new markets for exports, new sources of imports, and new investment opportunities.

On the other hand, these gains will not necessarily be shared equally by all regions. To assess the implications of this transition, we will focus on the consequences for trade patterns, capital markets, and the economies of specific regions. We will bring many different types of evidence to bear on these issues: depending on the context, we will resort to historical data (from the interwar period), econometric analysis, survey evidence, and a fair bit of a priori reasoning. We will try to make quantitative predictions wherever possible.

In all this, we will be trying to do precisely what Hirschman cautions against doing: predict the implications of the changes going on in East-

1

ern Europe and the Soviet Union—changes that themselves were unpre-
dictable. Hirschman's observation is an appropriately humbling starting
point. We will be guilty of committing many sins of the type that Hirschman has called in a different context "the fallacy of misplaced concrete-
ness." In the following chapters we will present estimates, having to do
with capital and trade flows, that are built on such shaky pyramids of
assumptions that they may as well have been drawn up as examples of
that particular fallacy. We will take a great many leaps of faith in assuming
what the economy of the region will look like in the future, and in extrapo-
lating from the trade patterns of the region in the interwar period.

Caution is made to be thrown to the wind. Hirschman's own skepticism
does not stop him from speculating—in the same article for which the
above lines serve as the opening—about the impact the Eastern European
revolutions might have on the developing world. For example, he suggests
that the developing countries may actually benefit from a period of neglect
by the outside world. Similarly, we shall not be deterred by modesty from
coming up with specific numbers. But the reader should bear in mind
that we are well aware of the range of uncertainty involved and of the
implausibility of some of our assumptions along the way. Our hope is to
frame the issues in as concrete a manner as possible, and to provide a
sound conceptual framework for further study. If some readers find our
quantitative predictions plausible also, all the better.

There is a sense in which Hirschman overstates the case for unpre-
dictability. It is true that the experts could not have foreseen the Eastern
European revolutions of 1989. But once those revolutions had taken
place and the new regimes had committed themselves to move toward
markets, some broad qualitative generalizations certainly became possible. Many of these generalizations have now become cliché: demand
for capital in the newly liberalizing countries will put upward pressure
on world interest rates; developing countries' access to international
capital markets will become more restricted; as the Council for Mutual
Economic Assistance (CMEA) collapses, the region will reorient its
trade toward the West; trade tensions will increase in many "sensitive"
sectors such as agriculture, steel, textiles, and clothing as producers in
the developing and the industrialized countries come under competitive
attack by new exporters in Eastern Europe.

There is a certain amount of truth in each one of these generalizations.
They all have important implications for policymaking in the interna-

tional arena and for the future of international economic relations. Our study aims to provide frameworks in which these issues can be addressed, as well as to provide guesses as to their likely magnitudes.

To be sure, the commitment to markets is still uncertain in some of the economies in transition. Most significantly, there appears to be a certain reversal recently in the Soviet Union in the importance attached to market-oriented reform. The speed with which reforms will be undertaken in Romania is still not clear, nor is the extent to which the opening in Yugoslavia will be sustained. There is doubt as to whether Yugoslavia and the Soviet Union will even continue as single political entities. It is possible that only Czechoslovakia, Hungary, and Poland—and an eastern Germany fully reunited with the Federal Republic—will fully integrate themselves with the world economy. Even within this group, continuing macroeconomic problems in Hungary and Poland may prevent them from playing a significant role anytime soon. We will discuss recent developments in each of these economies in greater detail below.

Our approach in estimating the trade and macroeconomic implications alike will be to start from what we call a "full catch-up" scenario: a long-run scenario in which Eastern Europe and the Soviet Union (EESU) will have been completely integrated into the world economy. This flight of fancy helps to focus our analysis and provides an outer bound on the magnitude of the potential impact. We then scale these magnitudes down by considering transitional issues and more likely developments.

There have been a number of recent studies on the implications for the world economy of developments in Eastern Europe (e.g., Congressional Budget Office [CBO] 1990 and Centre for Economic Policy Research [CEPR] 1990), and ours is naturally related to these. The CEPR study is particularly noteworthy, as it is the most comparable to the present one in its range, covering both trade and macroeconomic aspects. Many of our conclusions are similar also, although we are perhaps less sanguine about the trade implications for developing countries than are the authors of the CEPR report.[1]

---

1. The present study differs from the CEPR's mainly in providing more detailed trade projections, based in part on interwar trade experience; developing a more elaborate

A note about our terminology and coverage: In this study we will use the abbreviation EESU to refer to Eastern Europe and the Soviet Union as a group. References to "Eastern Europe" will generally mean Bulgaria, Czechoslovakia, the former East Germany, Hungary, Poland, Romania, and Yugoslavia. In the chapter on trade (chapter 2), however, the former East Germany will be generally left out of the analysis, unless we mention otherwise. "EE6" will refer to the countries of Eastern Europe except for the former East Germany.

As an introduction to our discussion, it is helpful to establish the size of the economies of EESU, individually and collectively, relative to the global economy and to set out our views on what economic transition will mean for these countries. Clearly, the smaller the region, the less will be the impact of developments in the region on the rest of the world. If little or no movement toward market systems occurs, or if these countries do not become increasingly integrated with the rest of the world, we would anticipate little effect from their "transition" on the global economy. Similarly, the greater the changes, and the greater the size of these economies at the outset, the greater the potential for substantial consequences arising from developments in the region. These issues are discussed in the remainder of this chapter.

How "Big" are Eastern Europe and the Soviet Union?

The main difficulty in estimating the relative size of EESU is that there are no generally agreed-upon measures of gross national product for the socialist and former socialist economies. (This difficulty is becoming less acute as the countries adopt standard Western methodologies and move toward market economies.) These countries have typically mea-

---

framework for macroeconomic implications; using econometric evidence to make interest rate predictions; paying greater attention to developing countries; providing survey evidence on private capital flows; and distinguishing between medium-run and long-run (full catch-up) scenarios. On the other hand, we pay less attention to the implications of German unification for exchange rates and the European Monetary System.

sured "net material product" instead. A central difference between this aggregate and standard measures of GNP is that net material product does not include the output of services. Also, official prices in planned economies do not accurately reflect the scarcity value of goods; hence output measures based on these prices do not reliably reflect the value of output. In countries such as Poland that have liberalized prices, prices have been quite volatile, and it may take some time for them to settle down. Finally, there is the problem of expressing GNP in a common currency, typically the US dollar. This is a difficult problem even for countries with realistic or market-determined exchange rates. It becomes still trickier in the case of EESU, some of whose currencies are not yet even convertible into dollars, much less subject to market determination of their exchange rates. Thus, analysts have used a variety of techniques to adjust nominal output estimates to create real output indices for EESU. We will consider a number of such estimates. We first look at population and per capita GNP and then turn to indicators of aggregate GNP.

Table 1.1 shows population in the region. The Eastern European countries excluding East Germany accounted for 2.3 percent of total world population in mid-1988. If one includes East Germany, this figure increases to 2.7 percent. This is approximately 42 percent of the population of the European Community. The Soviet Union's population is 286 million, or 5.6 percent of world population. This is about 16 percent greater than the US population and 88 percent the size of the EC population.

Table 1.2 presents a variety of estimates of per capita GNP for each country in the region. These estimates differ substantially from one another. For example, the estimate of Soviet GNP per capita reported by the US Central Intelligence Agency (CIA) is $9,230, which is 66 percent greater than the estimate by PlanEcon (a private consulting firm specializing in EESU economic affairs) and more than five times the recent estimate produced by a team of analysts from the International Monetary Fund (IMF), the World Bank, the Organization for Economic Cooperation and Development, the European Bank for Reconstruction and Development, and the European Commission. The CIA figure would put Soviet living standards at about 44 percent of the US level, while the IMF et al. (1990) put the figure at less than 10 percent of the

TABLE   1.1   **Eastern Europe and the Soviet Union: population, 1988**

Country	Population	
	Millions of persons	As a percentage of world population
Bulgaria	9.0	
Czechoslovakia	15.6	
Hungary	10.6	
Poland	38.0	
Romania	23.0	
Yugoslavia	23.6	
Total EE6	119.8	2.3
East Germany	16.6	
Soviet Union	286.4	5.6
Total EESU	422.8	8.2
Memoranda:		
European Community	324.4	6.3
World	5,147.0	100.0

Source: Central Intelligence Agency (1989).

US level. Overall, the estimates by Summers and Heston (1988) in table 1.2 are comparable to the estimates from PlanEcon. The CIA has recently revised downward its estimates for the Eastern European countries (but not for the Soviet Union), and these now look comparable to the PlanEcon ones also. (The CIA figures in table 1.2 are the revised ones.) However, World Bank figures, where available, are consistently below the other estimates.

It is difficult to determine which set of estimates most accurately reflects output per capita in these countries. The CIA figures for the Soviet Union appear much too high relative to impressions of actual production and living standards. Current estimates for the former East Germany suggest that its output per capita was at best half that in the former West Germany. At the same time, the World Bank figures appear

TABLE 1.2 **Eastern Europe and the Soviet Union: alternative estimates of per capita GNP** (in dollars)[a]

Country	Heston-Summers (1985)	PlanEcon (1988)	CIA (1989)	World Bank (1988)
Bulgaria	5,113	5,630	5,690	n.a.
Czechoslovakia	7,424	7,600	7,900	n.a.
East Germany	8,740	9,360	9,670	n.a.
Hungary	5,765	6,490	6,090	2,460
Poland	4,913	5,450	4,560	1,860
Romania	4,273	4,120	3,440	n.a.
Soviet Union	6,266	5,550	9,230	1,735
Yugoslavia	5,063	4,900	5,460	2,520
Memoranda:				
West Germany			15,250	18,480
United States			20,890	19,840

n.a. = not available.

a. The Heston-Summers figures are in 1980 international dollars. See Summers and Heston (1988) for details. Other data are in current dollars.

Sources: Summers and Heston (1988); *PlanEcon Report,* various issues; Central Intelligence Agency (1990). World Bank (1990b) and IMF et al. (1990).

to us somewhat low overall. These figures suggest that the Soviet Union and Poland have living standards below the average for the middle-income developing countries—about half the level in South Korea, for example, and comparable with Mexico. In our discussion, we will use as a benchmark the PlanEcon estimates, which are similar to the Heston-Summers and CIA figures (except for the CIA's estimate for the Soviet Union).

What do these figures imply about the overall size of these economies? Table 1.3 shows two sets of estimates. One uses the CIA data. The second combines PlanEcon estimates for EESU with World Bank data for the rest of the world economy. The main difference between the two sets of estimates relates to the size of the Soviet economy. According to the CIA figures, the Soviet Union accounted for 13.2

TABLE 1.3   **Eastern Europe and the Soviet Union: alternative estimates of total GNP**

Country	CIA (1989)		PlanEcon (1988)	
	Billions of dollars	Percentage of world GNP	Billions of dollars	Percentage of world GNP
Bulgaria	51.2		50.7	
Czechoslovakia	123.2		118.6	
Hungary	64.6		68.8	
Poland	172.4		207.1	
Romania	79.8		94.8	
Yugoslavia	129.5		115.6	
Total EE6	620.7	3.1	655.6	3.5
East Germany	159.5		155.4	
Soviet Union	2,663.7	13.2	1,589.5	8.6
Total EESU	3,443.9	17.0	2,400.5	12.9
Memorandum: world GNP	20,200.0		18,584[a]	11.20

a. PlanEcon does not quote a "world GNP" figure. This number is the World Bank total 1988 GNP of all reporting countries ($16,434.6 billion), less the World Bank estimate of GNP for Hungary, Poland, and Yugoslavia ($156.1 billion), plus $2,400.5 billion, which is the PlanEcon estimate for EESU GNP.

Sources: PlanEcon Report, various issues; Central Intelligence Agency (1990a).

percent of the world economy in 1989, whereas the alternative estimate (for 1988) is only 8.6 percent. The Eastern European countries (excluding East Germany) together accounted for 3.1 percent and 3.5 percent of the world economy under the two sets of figures, respectively. Eastern Europe and the Soviet Union together accounted for 17.0 percent or 12.9 percent of world GNP, depending on the estimate used. According to the lower PlanEcon figures (which we will use in the rest of this analysis), total production for Eastern Europe (including East Germany) is a bit more than $800 billion, or a fifth of the European Commu-

TABLE   1.4   Eastern Europe and the Soviet Union: merchandise exports,
              1988

Country	Billions of dollars	As a percentage of GNP[a]	As a percentage of world exports
Bulgaria	17.3	34.1	0.64
Czechoslovakia[b]	23.0	19.4	0.85
East Germany[b]	31.2	20.0	1.16
Hungary	10.0	14.5	0.37
Poland	14.0	6.8	0.52
Romania	12.6	13.3	0.47
Soviet Union	110.5	7.0	4.10
Yugoslavia	12.8	11.1	0.48
Total EESU	231.4	9.6	8.59
Memorandum:			
West Germany	322.6	26.8	

a. GNP figures from PlanEcon.

b. Data are for 1987.

Sources: PlanEcon Report, various issues; World Bank (1990b), and Economic Commission for Europe (1990).

nity's production, and about the same as Italy's production ($825 billion in 1988). Soviet output is about $1.6 trillion, equivalent to about 40 percent of EC production or a third of US production.

Table 1.4 shows total merchandise exports from the region. These figures include both exports to the ruble area and hard-currency exports. They are sensitive to the accuracy of prices used to value ruble exports. Eastern Europe as a whole exported $121 billion worth of goods in 1988, which is about 4.5 percent of total world merchandise exports. Soviet merchandise exports were $111 billion in 1988, about a third of West Germany's exports and about 4 percent of the world total. In chapter 2 we will discuss the region's trade in some detail, including the likely developments in the volume and direction of trade.

TABLE   1.5   Eastern Europe and the Soviet Union: external debt, 1989

Country	Billions of dollars	Percentage of world total
Bulgaria	9.0	
Czechoslovakia	6.5	
Hungary	18.5	
Poland	40.0	
Romania	1.0	
Yugoslavia	17.7	
Total EE6	92.7	7.1
East Germany	20.0	
Soviet Union	46.0	3.5
Total EESU	158.7	12.2
Memorandum: world external debt	1,300.0	100.0

Sources: Debt stocks for Eastern Europe and Soviet Union are from the OECD Secretariat. The world debt stock figure is from the World Bank.

Many countries in the region have accumulated large external debts. Table 1.5 shows the magnitude of these debt stocks. The Soviet Union and Poland have the largest debts, but Hungary's and Bulgaria's debts are much larger compared to the size of their economies. Eastern Europe as a group had accumulated more than $110 billion in debt by 1989—about the same as Brazil.

Transition to a Market Economy: General Issues

The transition to a market economy involves certain basic elements that are common in all cases. It will be useful to discuss these elements briefly, not in order to assess the relative merits of alternative strategies or to advance an "ideal" strategy, but to set out the general issues

T A B L E   1.6   Elements of transition to a market economy

Macroeconomic stabilization
 Sustainable monetary and fiscal policies
 Competitive exchange rate

Price reform
 Domestic price liberalization
 Trade liberalization
 Currency convertibility for current account transactions

Structural and institutional reforms
 Hard budget constraints for firms
 Reform of the legal system—including property rights protection
 Private-sector development—including privatization
 Reform of the banking system and financial intermediaries
 Expansion of capital infrastructure
 Development of a social safety net

involved so as to facilitate discussion of what we believe is likely to occur in each country.

In fact, there is broad agreement on the major steps that must be undertaken in order to transform a socialist economy into a market economy. The major disagreements focus on the appropriate sequencing and the appropriate speed with which these measures should be implemented. Much of this controversy is linked in turn to concern over the costs of transition. For more complete analyses of these transitional issues, the reader is referred to Genberg (1990), Hinds (1990), Portes (1990), and Williamson (1991). Table 1.6 lists the key issues that must be addressed in any transition. We have divided them into three categories: macroeconomic stabilization measures, price reform, and structural and institutional reforms.

It is widely agreed that a precondition for most other economic reforms is macroeconomic stability. Stability here means balancing total domestic demand with total domestic production so that the price level, overall, is relatively constant and predictable, and that the country does not need to borrow from abroad beyond its future capacity to service its debt. Absent such stability, it is extremely difficult for prices to act as effective market signals—a central aspect of a healthy market economy.

Essentially, achieving macroeconomic stability entails establishing and maintaining a sustainable fiscal policy—typically with the budget at or near balance—and control over the growth of the money supply. Budget control will generally require elimination of many of the price subsidies that proliferate under extensive systems of government price controls. Thus, it is tied to liberalization of the pricing system. Because wages typically make up a large share of government expenditures, bringing a deficit down usually also involves an explicit agreement on wages. Over the medium run, tax reform will also be essential, among other reasons because government revenues are intimately tied to the system of price controls in these economies. In addition to reduction of fiscal deficits, two key problems that have compromised the ability of monetary authorities to control money growth have been the proliferation of interfirm credits, and in some cases (notably Yugoslavia) regional banks' ability to print money independently of the national central bank.

Price reform entails dismantling the complex system of centrally controlled prices and allowing them to reflect relative scarcities and tastes. Many analysts believe that the most effective means of establishing a sensible set of relative prices—at least for tradeable goods and services—is to "import" prices from the world economy through trade liberalization. This is essentially the route that has been followed by both the former East Germany and Poland. Of course, opening the economy can lead to large external imbalances if macroeconomic policies are unsustainable, or if the exchange rate is substantially overvalued. A key difference in the paths taken by these two countries is that Poland began with a relatively undervalued currency, whereas East Germany adopted an exchange rate that substantially overvalued its currency. This appears to be a major factor in explaining the much greater collapse in economic activity in the latter.

Finally, there are a variety of institutional and structural changes that are central to creating a healthy market economy. We mention here only a few from a long list. First, enterprises have little incentive to respond to market signals when their outlays are simply financed by subsidies from the government. Thus, it is crucial to establish "hard" budget constraints for firms in order to weed out those that will be insolvent at realistic prices. This step is also critical in enabling the government to balance its budget. Governments must also take steps to develop the private sector, including the elimination of restrictions— or red tape—on the establishment of private firms, and the privatization of state-owned enterprises. Also key is the development of financial intermediaries that can effectively channel domestic saving into needed investment projects. Last but not least, extensive legal reforms are needed, including legislation to protect private property.

The Transition in Individual Economies

A central point in our discussion will be to stress the heterogeneity of the countries in the region. The countries differ in a number of important respects. We have seen that they range considerably in size. There are also differences in their sectoral composition, with agricultural production accounting for a large share of the total in countries such as Romania, and others, such as Czechoslovakia, considerably more industrial. In 1990, the countries of the region were at very different starting points in terms of how much relative prices and the allocation of resources differed from the outcomes that would be expected with functioning markets. For example, Hungary had been liberalizing gradually for years, whereas other countries had barely started to initiate economic reforms. Finally, there are also differences in the prevailing political and social situations, which can be a central force in either pushing economic reform forward or bringing other difficult issues to the forefront of the policy agenda. These conditions also contribute to the extreme uncertainty that now exists about the future course of events in some of the countries.

This section briefly discusses the economic situation and efforts toward market-oriented reform in each of the countries.[2] Although each

---

2. There have been many detailed analyses of economic policy and performance in individual countries. These include Lipton and Sachs (1990) and Blanchard and Layard (1990) on Poland, Kornai (1990) on Hungary, Burda (1990) on German unification, and

has unique features, it is useful to identify a few broad patterns. Two countries, Poland and Yugoslavia, launched ambitious stabilization and reform programs at the beginning of 1990 to combat hyperinflations. We examine the Polish experience at some length below, as its radical program of stabilization and liberalization may well hold important lessons for the other countries as well. Two other countries, Hungary and Czechoslovakia, are in the midst of more gradual liberalization programs. However, considerable progress has already been made in Hungary, and the tempo of change accelerated in Czechoslovakia in early 1991. Bulgaria and Romania also adopted radical reforms in 1991, but the outcomes remain in doubt. There is considerably less certainty about whether—and if so what type—of reform programs will be implemented in the Soviet Union. In contrast, the former East Germany is well on its way toward integration with the former West Germany. Although the transition in the former East Germany continues to be a difficult one, its direction—toward establishment of a market economy, fully integrated with the West—is irreversible. In the discussion below, we focus on economic policy and performance.

POLAND

Poland is in the midst of implementing the most ambitious and comprehensive reform program (save for that in the former East Germany) in the region. Perhaps the main impetus behind Poland's attempt at "shock therapy" was the soaring inflation rate that exceeded 50 percent per month at the end of 1989. By then the havoc from hyperinflation had clearly supplanted shortages and inefficiencies caused by central planning as the overriding policy concern. But in addition to macroeconomic stabilization measures, the reform program has liberalized prices and taken steps to address the structural and institutional developments necessary to establish a market economy.

Commission of the European Communities (1990) on the Soviet Union. Williamson (1991), Economic Commission of Europe (1990), CIA (1990b), and *PlanEcon Report* (various issues) provide discussions of all of the countries.

Price stabilization was the first priority of the Solidarity-led government that came to power in August 1989. The program it implemented on 1 January 1990 included tight fiscal and monetary policies, a large devaluation of the zloty (from 3,800 to the dollar in November 1989 to 9,500 to the dollar) to establish a competitive (and temporarily fixed) exchange rate, and virtually full current account convertibility. Government subsidies to producers and consumers were cut, and wage increase ceilings were announced (with tax penalties for firms that granted increases above the ceiling). Although controls on capital transactions remain, enterprises and consumers can purchase unlimited amounts of foreign exchange for current account transactions purposes. Individuals are allowed to maintain accounts denominated in foreign currency.

The government also implemented a major trade liberalization, eliminating virtually all quantitative restrictions and relying exclusively on tariffs for trade protection. It has taken steps toward private-sector development and has announced plans to privatize state enterprises. One thousand of the 7,600 existing state enterprises, accounting for perhaps half of industrial production, are to be privatized over a two-year period. However, structural and institutional developments will necessarily move more slowly than the macroeconomic stabilization.

What have been the results of these measures? In some respects, the outcome has been extremely positive. Inflation fell from 78 percent per month in January 1990 to 1.8 percent in August. Although inflation has since increased, the threat of hyperinflation appears to have been substantially reduced. The budget deficit (3.6 percent of GDP in 1989) has been reversed to a surplus (about 4 percent of GDP in 1990), and money growth has been kept in check. Price and trade liberalization means that the prices of most traded goods are comparable to those in the West, and Poland's private sector and trade with the West are both booming.

On the external front, Poland has large surpluses in both hard-currency and ruble trade. In particular, exports to the West have increased substantially, indeed more than had been anticipated. Hard-currency exports rose by more than 25 percent in volume terms during 1990, after stagnating in 1989. Although some of this increase is the counterpart to sharp declines in domestic demand and in demand from

Poland's traditional CMEA trading partners, Polish exports have proved quite responsive to the large real devaluation.

Private-sector output is estimated to have risen by 25 percent. Although still accounting for a small share of industry, the private sector has shown encouraging signs of growth, from about 4.8 percent of the total in 1989 to 6.8 percent in 1990. However, these official figures may substantially understate private-sector activity, as other data show 17 percent of the industrial labor force employed in the private sector, and most observers conclude that private firms are substantially more efficient than the large public enterprises.

The decline in total output has been somewhat more pronounced than many anticipated. GDP appears to have fallen by more than 18 percent during 1990. This drop is concentrated in the large state-owned enterprises and in construction.

It is difficult to estimate the effect the reform program has had on real incomes. The official estimate of a 30 percent drop is likely to be exaggerated. Goods and services that formerly were sold at controlled prices make up a large share of the consumption basket. The low official price increases of these commodities under the old regime, even when there were shortages, meant that real income measures overstated true living standards. With liberalization, prices of these goods have soared, but in many cases availability has also risen.

Nonetheless, it is clear that the Polish economy is in the midst of a severe squeeze. It is unclear whether more bad news is right around the corner, and if so, whether a deepening of the recession would significantly unravel the apparent public support for the reform efforts. It is also unclear, for example, whether the surprising results of the national elections in November-December 1990 suggest that public support is already eroding. In that election Prime Minister Tadeusz Mazowiecki, whose administration introduced the radical reform package, was ousted in the first round of voting.

Poland's gross external debt rose to $42.5 billion by mid-1990. About $10.3 billion is owed to foreign commercial banks, and the remaining three-quarters of the debt to Western governments. Poland did not pay any interest or principal on its commercial debts in 1990. In March 1991, the Paris Club agreed to a reduction of at least 50 percent in Poland's debt to Western governments—the largest debt reduction provided so far to any debtor. In addition, the US government has announced its intention of providing debt reduction of 70 percent.

Overall, then, Poland appears well along the path toward market development and full integration with the West. Structural and institutional developments are likely to take a number of years, but the government appears strongly committed to continuing along its chosen path. Political developments or public unrest could still derail the reform program, but many of the steps already taken, including the deregulation of prices, are irreversible. In most respects, the Polish economy could already be classified as a market economy.

YUGOSLAVIA

Yugoslavia, like Poland, implemented an impressive stabilization program at the beginning of 1990 to combat hyperinflation. However, its underlying economic situation is quite different in a number of respects. First, Yugoslavia was closer to a market economy in 1989 than was Poland. It was not a CMEA member. It was an observer at the Organization for Economic Cooperation and Development, and it has had stronger ties to the West for several decades. A second difference is that Yugoslavia has had a much stronger external position than Poland. More aggressive exchange rate adjustment (to offset high rates of inflation) has kept external balances in surplus. For this reason Yugoslavia did not accumulate a large external debt.

Also, the underlying causes of Yugoslavia's hyperinflation were somewhat different and arguably more difficult to control. In Poland, unsustainable national macroeconomic policies were a major problem, as money was created to finance a runaway central-government deficit. In Yugoslavia, the national monetary authorities lost control of the money supply precisely because of a lack of central authority. Regional banks could print money independently, and state enterprises could extend credit to one another.

The centerpiece of the Yugoslav stabilization has therefore been to establish a single authority for the control of money creation. Although the new regime appears to be working, there remain concerns that ethnic tensions could once again erupt in runaway inflation—especially as regional governments must cope with rising unemployment due to austere federal policies, and as the pressures for expansionary regional policies mount. In view of the centrifugal political forces at work, the ability of the national monetary authorities to keep money growth—and inflation—in check remains extremely uncertain.

HUNGARY

Hungary began to dismantle its system of central planning and controls some twenty years ago. Although many of the steps were at best partially successful, by 1989 the Hungarian economy was substantially less distorted and more liberal than, for example, the Polish economy. Macroeconomic balances have also been kept in check, so that no severe austerity measures are required merely to establish stability. There is a general sense that the Hungarian economy—perhaps even more than the Czechoslovak economy—is well placed for a successful transition to a market system. PlanEcon, for example, argues that Hungarian entrepreneurs have the most developed business sense in the region, making Hungary a more favorable environment for private-sector development and foreign investment than either Poland or Czechoslovakia.

However, there are some less favorable aspects of the Hungarian situation as well. First, although the economy is generally viewed as more developed than those of either Poland or Yugoslavia, its capital stock has been poorly maintained and is extremely outdated. Real gross fixed capital formation declined in 9 out of 11 years from 1980 through 1990. Second, Hungary has an extremely heavy external debt burden and has one of the highest levels of debt per capita in the world. Unlike in Poland, most of this debt is owed to commercial banks. To date, all debt obligations have been met without rescheduling, but these obligations pose serious potential difficulties for the future.

The Hungarian government has been pursuing a gradualist program of economic reform. About 90 percent of all prices have been liberalized, and steps have been taken to encourage private-sector development. Privatization of state enterprises is under way. The first privatization offering, in June 1990, attracted some domestic interest—

and stronger-than-anticipated foreign interest. The forint was devalued moderately in early 1990 and then pegged to a basket of currencies. The government has announced its intention to make the forint convertible for current account transactions in 1991.

The Hungarian economy has also gone into a recession, although it has not been as deep as the downturn in Poland or the former East Germany. GDP declined by 7 percent in 1990, with domestic demand falling 10 percent and exports on balance expanding. Consumption has fallen to its level of 1979, and gross fixed capital formation to its level of 1974. On the supply side, a severe drought has led to a 7 percent contraction of agricultural output. The output of large firms (i.e., those with 50 or more employees) contracted by 10 percent in the first half of 1990, while private-sector production (primarily by small firms) expanded by at least 25 percent. Inflation has also accelerated, from 7 percent on average during 1981–88 to 30 percent in 1990.

Hungary's external debt remains a major concern, with annual debt obligations of about $2.4 billion. Official foreign-exchange reserves have already been reduced substantially to keep the country current on its debt obligations. The existing debt has been selling at a modest discount in secondary markets (12 percent in October 1990). Foreign investment inflows have been increasing, but slowly: foreign direct investment rose from less than $200 million in 1989 to slightly more than $300 million in 1990.

There are a number of uncertainties facing Hungary. First, how will it resolve growing difficulties in its external finances? In particular, will the continued attempts to service the heavy debt burden either slow down progress in liberalizing the domestic economy, or lead to further curtailment of capital formation, or both? And will the gradual approach to reform run out of steam if the public becomes concerned about rising unemployment?

CZECHOSLOVAKIA

Czechoslovakia is the most developed economy in the region, with a per capita income one-third the US level. The country has maintained tight macroeconomic policies and has the strongest position among the region's economies in terms of external finance. It has just become a member of both the IMF and the World Bank. Its gross hard-currency debt is just $7 billion, and some estimates suggest that it is a net creditor.

So far, the new government headed by President Václav Havel has successfully maintained tight fiscal and monetary policies. In fact, the overall budget is in surplus, and domestic credit expansion has been kept within the range announced last year of − 1 percent to + 2 percent. During 1990, substantial progress was made toward a unified exchange rate, as the gaps between the official commercial exchange rate, an intermediate tourist rate, and the free auction rate narrowed. Beginning in 1991, the government moved toward convertibility for the koruna. The IMF has recently approved a Stand-by Arrangement.

Czechoslovak economic performance has been the strongest in the region during the transition period. GDP declined by only 3.4 percent in 1990, compared with 7 percent in Hungary and more than 18 percent in Poland. The decline reflects drops in both industrial production and agriculture. Fixed capital formation, however, appears to have increased in real terms. Unemployment rose to 1 percent, although it is expected to reach 5 percent in 1991. Inflation rose to about 30 percent as many prices were liberalized. Further price liberalization is to take place in 1991. As in the rest of the region, there has been a major shift in trade flows toward the West.

Overall, Czechoslovakia appears to be well placed for market development and integration with the West. The main wild card is the strong ethnic tensions between the Czechs and the Slovaks, which could threaten future reform efforts.

ROMANIA

The Romanian economy is in very poor shape following a decade of extreme austerity under President Nicolae Ceausescu. Real income is estimated to have dropped by 15 percent during 1980–88 as domestic demand was curtailed to free resources for repayment of external debts. It is difficult to assess the current economic situation because of extremely poor and often inconsistent data. (For example, new official data suggest that agriculture in this largely unindustrialized country accounts for just 12 percent of GDP—below the share in Hungary!) The new government under Ion Iliescu has announced its commitment to establishing free markets, and extensive reforms are under consideration. But few steps have been taken to date. The country enters the transition without a debt problem, as practically all of Romania's external debt was repaid under the Ceausescu regime.

Following the collapse of the Ceausescu dictatorship, Romanian consumption surged. Increased imports pushed the current account from surplus into deficit. PlanEcon estimates that GDP dropped by more than 15 percent in 1990, following a 7 percent decline in 1989. The economic situation has clearly deteriorated. Romania's prospects for transition remain extremely uncertain.

BULGARIA

Until recently there was little consensus among leading political groups in Bulgaria regarding the way to proceed to a market economy. The Communists remain in power, although they have nominally turned over the design of the economic program to the parliamentary opposition. After a drop in domestic output of 11 percent and a rise in inflation to 60 percent in 1990, the government adopted a number of important reforms at the beginning of 1991. Most consumer and producer prices were liberalized; interest rates were raised; import licensing was abolished for most goods; budgetary expenditures and subsidies were cut; and the exchange rate was unified and floated. In March 1991, Bulgaria was granted a 12-month Stand-by Agreement with the IMF (which it had joined in September 1990).

The country suffers from deep-seated structural problems inherited from more than four decades of socialism, as well as large macroeconomic imbalances. Practically all of Bulgarian output is generated in the state sector. Among all the Eastern European economies, Bulgaria is the most dependent on the Soviet Union. Despite the encouraging recent developments, the macroeconomic situation is likely to remain precarious. The country's relatively large external debt is not being serviced. The move to dollar pricing of oil, the collapse of the CMEA trade arrangements, and the difficulties faced by the Soviet economy will hit Bulgaria particularly hard. The magnitude of the problems faced by the economy and the lack of political consensus both suggest that the road ahead will be very bumpy indeed.

SOVIET UNION

The overall economic situation in the Soviet Union has also deteriorated, and recent events call into question the central government's commitment to market-oriented economic reform. The struggle for independence of the republics further increases the uncertainty regarding the economic transition.

Some policy reforms have been implemented. For example, restrictions on foreign investors have been liberalized, and foreign trade has been decentralized, although licenses are still required to conduct foreign activities. However, real output has declined—officially by 2 percent in 1990, but most Western estimates suggest a decline of at least 5 percent. Money growth has accelerated, but prices remain controlled. The government continues to respond to growing shortages and social unrest by readjusting—not dismantling—output targets and price controls. It has grown increasingly concerned about evidence of a growing ruble overhang, as households continue to accumulate currency holdings. In response, in February 1990 the government declared large-denomination bills worthless (beyond a very limited quota per person), wiping out the saving of many households.

On the external side, the Soviet Union's deficit with its former CMEA trade partners has widened, and its previous trade surplus with the West has turned sharply into deficit. Foreign-exchange reserves have been drawn down sharply, and Western banks appear to be reducing their exposure. Although a new exchange rate ($0.60 to the ruble) for most commercial transactions has been announced, this rate appears to overvalue the currency. Hungary and Czechoslovakia value the transferable ruble at $0.40 to $0.45, while Poland values it at about $0.22.

Overall, few signs point toward a major economic transition in the Soviet Union within the next few years.

EAST GERMANY

The integration of the former East and West Germanys provides a stark contrast to the uncertain economic reform attempts in the Soviet Union. The East German route has been an unambiguous shock therapy. It has also entailed a collapse of economic activity in eastern Germany, which is eroding political support for the transition measures.

On 1 July 1990, East Germany adopted the West German deutsche mark as its legal tender, and on 3 October 1990 the two Germanys were formally reunited. Reunification has meant that the former East Germany has chosen to introduce wholesale the Federal Republic's laws, regulations, and economic and political institutions in a relatively short period of time. Political unification also indicates there can be little doubt that the transition in the former East Germany is permanent and irreversible.

Currency conversion in East Germany involved an exchange of East German marks (ostmarks) for deutsche marks at a 1:1 ratio for flow prices (e.g., wages, pensions, and goods prices), and a 1.8:1 ratio on average for asset prices (e.g., bank deposits and other financial claims). The immediate effect of economic unification was a severe depression, as much of existing production in East Germany became uncompetitive with the West overnight. Owing to their lower productivity and the shoddy quality of their goods, many East German enterprises went bankrupt and unemployment skyrocketed. Current estimates put East German industrial production at half its level prior to unification. A German Unity Fund has been established to mobilize and transfer resources to eastern Germany, in an attempt to cushion what has become an extremely difficult transition to markets.

In addition, privatization remains a major roadblock. State-owned companies in the former East Germany (some 7,900 of them) have been turned over to a trust agency of the German Ministry of Finance, the Treuhandanstalt, whose job it is to find private buyers for the vast majority of these enterprises. The privatization process has so far moved slowly.

Despite these problems, the East German transition benefits from several special circumstances. First, the political dimension of the transition solidifies the commitment to markets and makes the prospects for reversal unlikely. However, political pressures to slow the transition have been growing. Second, the budgetary resources made available by the federal government allow for sizable financial transfers to the East and should enable the region to maintain higher wages than would be justified on competitiveness grounds alone. Third, the adoption of the Federal Republic's legal institutions and its political stability renders eastern Germany a potentially much more hospitable environment for foreign investors. In all these respects, the former East Germany's transition is likely to be qualitatively different from that in the rest of EESU.

As this brief review makes clear, the prospects for transition to market economies in EESU are very uneven. The former East Germany is at one end of the spectrum. Its transition has gone too far to be derailed. However, adjustment promises to be very costly. In our view, Poland is next in the sense that some type of a market economy now appears inevitable. Hungary and Czechoslovakia have implemented many of the necessary steps to date, but perhaps their transitions have greater potential for stalling. Both of their economies are stronger overall than the Polish economy. From a foreign investor's point of view, they may provide the better risks. The Yugoslav transition may already have gone off track, and its prognosis is more difficult to call than those of Hungary or Czechoslovakia. Romania and Bulgaria appear to have embraced a market economy as their goal but are at the very early stages of implementing a transition. Finally, at the other end of the spectrum is the Soviet Union, which has yet to articulate clearly what type of economy it envisages.

Even if all of the necessary policies are implemented, it will take time for these economies to undergo this major transition. Thus, our discussion in the remaining chapters will distinguish between the optimistic long-run scenario of full transition and integration into the world economy, and what we view as the more realistic scenario of partial and uneven development.

A Road Map and Some Conclusions

The next two chapters discuss the trade and macroeconomic implications of the integration of EESU into the world economy. In chapter 2 our focus will be on trade flows. We will ask the following questions:

How much, if at all, is the region's openness to external trade likely to increase as a consequence of liberalization? What will happen to the overall volume of trade of the region under different scenarios with respect to income growth? What will the direction of trade look like? What will the product composition of trade look like? Finally, but most importantly, what do these likely developments imply for the economies of other regions of the world?

The opening of EESU to the international economy is a welcome development for the world as a whole. The expansion of trade with EESU will generate new markets for exports from both the industrialized and the developing countries, as well as provide new sources for imports. The analysis in chapter 2 provides some quantitative magnitudes for these effects. The analysis (part of the methodology of which is described in appendix A) also shows that the effects are unlikely to be spread uniformly across all countries and regions. The trade impact of EESU transformation will be felt mainly in Western Europe; the effects on the United States, Japan, and the developing countries will be small and indirect. Our quantitative analysis points to a substantial redirection of EESU trade toward Western Europe over the next few years. Although this should be a source of economic gain to Western Europe as a whole, we will also argue that the implied market penetration levels of EESU in the European Community are too high to justify remaining sanguine about the trade policy implications. Absorbing the impact of the opening of EESU, without erecting trade barriers or shifting the burden onto non-European countries, will be a major challenge for EC trade policy in the years ahead.

In chapter 3 we will turn to capital flows and macroeconomic implications. The questions we will ask are the following: How much capital, private and official, is likely to flow into EESU? How do these magnitudes compare with calculations based on catch-up scenarios? How much should we expect world interest rates to rise in response to the additional demands placed on capital markets? What are the implications for macroeconomic performance and policy in developing and developed countries, and in particular in the United States and the European Community?

We conclude in chapter 3 that the likely net flows of capital into the region fall in the range of $30 billion to $90 billion per year for the next five years. We refer in this chapter to the results of a survey we conducted of large Western firms (discussed in more detail in appendix C). These results indicate strong interest in the region: our respondents anticipate a tripling or quadrupling of the EESU share in their investment portfolios over the next five years. However, the implied totals remain small, given the small initial base.

We also report in chapter 3 on an econometric exercise aimed at quantifying the trade-off between increases in world interest rates and reductions in net resource transfers to developing countries. We find that if all of the increase in flows to EESU comes at the expense of reduced transfers to developing countries, the drop in the investment–GDP ratio in these countries would be in the range of 0.8 to 2.4 percentage points. If instead none of it does, global real interest rates would rise by between 1 and 3 percentage points. The likely outcome lies somewhere between these two extreme scenarios.

For the OECD countries as a whole, we will argue that the macroeconomic effects of the increase in EESU demand for capital are positive (these issues are spelled out formally in appendix B). These countries should receive an expansionary boost on balance, and should grow faster thanks to the higher-yielding investment opportunities opened up in the East. However, within the OECD, the situations of the United States and the European Commuity are quite different. The main beneficiaries of the region's capital rehabilitation will be the Western European countries. For the Community, therefore, the increase in net exports will likely offset the negative interest rate effect on aggregate demand. For the United States, the opposite is likely to occur. A similar asymmetry may also prevail between the effects on Germany on the one hand, and on some of the other EC members on the other.

2 Consequences for International Trade

We examine in this chapter some likely developments on the trade front. There are at least three kinds of questions that we need to address. First, how much, if at all, are the aggregate trade volumes of the countries of Eastern Europe and the Soviet Union likely to increase? Second, will there be much alteration in the geographical composition of their trade, and if so, what will the new patterns look like? Third, what will the product composition of their trade look like? As we indicated in chapter 1, our initial focus is the very long-run outcome in which EESU will have become thoroughly integrated into the world economy. We try to predict the volume and direction of trade that will prevail at the end of these countries' transition to a market economy. But we also discuss shorter-run issues and the more likely outcomes.

EESU's trade during the 1990s will be shaped by two main developments. The first of these is the progressive liberalization of these countries' trade regimes. Poland has already traveled far along this road, having eliminated practically all quantitative restrictions on trade with the West and rendered the zloty convertible on current account. A more gradual process of trade liberalization has already made substantial progress in Hungary, and a Poland-like transition has begun in Czechoslovakia in 1991. The other countries are much behind but are likely to move in the same direction, if more haltingly and hesitatingly.

The second significant development is the official dismantling of CMEA trading arrangements beginning in 1991. This has put an end to the complex bilateralism that long dominated these countries' trade relations with each other, as well as the implicit pattern of subsidization of manufactured goods at the expense of natural resources and energy. These trade relations will now become decentralized and market-oriented, and in principle no different from trade with the West. These two developments will reinforce each other in making Eastern Europe's trade patterns look more and more like those of market-oriented countries at similar levels of development.

What will that mean in practice? We can identify two main implications. First, to the extent that socialist planning has repressed trade, liberalization will lead to an overall expansion of these countries' trade. This volume-of-trade effect could come about either through an increase in openness—the share of domestic output that is exported or imported—or through an expansion of output. Second, once CMEA is done away with, Eastern European countries are likely to trade less with each other and more with the rest of the world, and particularly with Western Europe. This is the direction-of-trade effect.

Both these developments will open new markets for Western exporters. Countries that are best positioned in terms of supplying these new markets will be the beneficiaries. Developed countries, and Western Europe in particular, are likely to dominate this group. On the other hand, countries that are close competitors with Eastern European exports could lose out. We suggest that the middle-income countries and the newly industrializing countries are likely to be in this second group, since their level of development and their comparative advantage patterns are closest to those of the Eastern European countries. But by the same token this redirection of trade could also have important adverse effects in Western markets in certain "sensitive" sectors such as textiles, clothing, and agriculture, where firms in successfully reforming Eastern European countries could become formidable competitors.

Hence, taken together, the volume-of-trade and direction-of-trade effects will have predictable consequences for the terms of trade and the market shares of other countries. In fact, some of these changes are already in evidence for countries that have made considerable progress in economic reform. As we shall describe in greater detail at the end of the chapter, Poland and Hungary have experienced a sharp rise in exports to the West. Their trade with the former CMEA members—and with the Soviet Union in particular—has either stagnated or been drastically curtailed.

As we mentioned above, our initial focus is on a full catch-up scenario in which EESU complete a successful transition and become "like" developed market economies in three respects: openness, direction of trade, and income levels.[1] It is important to stress, however, that even if the transitions are successful, this scenario is relevant only in the longer run—say, in 20 years. In particular, even with very rapid growth rates, it would take many years for real incomes in EESU to reach the levels enjoyed in Western Europe. But it is conceivable that liberalization will result in a much quicker transformation of trade patterns (in terms of openness and geographical composition of trade). Thus, we also consider a scenario that combines little income growth with substantial liberalization of trade patterns; this scenario would appear to be more relevant over the medium run.

The next two sections of this chapter will provide some rough quantitative estimates related to the volume-of-trade and direction-of-trade effects following the integration of EESU into the world economy. After that we will pull these results together and present various scenarios for trade volumes and their potential impact on the European Community, Germany, and the United States in the medium and the long run. We will then turn to the likely comparative advantage pattern of EESU. We will also briefly discuss recent trends in the trade of two countries, Poland and Hungary, that have traveled furthest among this group on the road to a market economy. We summarize our main conclusions at the end of the chapter.

Volume of Trade

What will happen to the overall volume of EESU trade as these countries liberalize and integrate themselves into the world economy? There are two parts to this question. First, given estimates of output levels,

---

1. In other words, we are decomposing exports from EESU country i to trade partner j (X_{ij}) into three components:

$$X_{ij} = (X_i / Y_i)(X_{ij}/X_i)Y_i,$$

where X_i stands for total exports of country i, and Y_i its level of income. The first component here is openness, the share of output that is exported. The second is the direction of trade, the share of country i's exports that goes to country j. The third effect is the income effect, which scales the value of exports up or down.

TABLE 2.1   Eastern Europe[a] and the Soviet Union: share of CMEA
countries in total trade, 1988 (percentages)

Country	Exports	Imports
Bulgaria	80.8	73.8
Czechoslovakia	73.1	72.6
East Germany	60.9	62.0
Hungary	44.6	43.8
Poland	40.7	40.6
Romania	40.9	58.4
Total Eastern Europe CMEA members	60.4	61.9
Soviet Union	48.9	54.1

a. Excluding Yugoslavia, which was not a CMEA member.
Source: Economic Commission for Europe. ECE Secretariat estimates are used for Romania because of the absence of national data.

how much will openness increase, if at all? Second, what is likely to happen to output levels? We address each in turn.

OPENNESS

It is not clear that liberalization will necessarily make EESU more open. Although the rigid quantitative controls on prices and production that characterized socialist planning have discouraged foreign trade with the West, the CMEA regime did aim at establishing a "socialist" division of labor among the member countries.[2] This would tend to increase trade. The resulting interdependence is reflected in the high level of intra–CMEA trade, which ranges from 41 percent for Poland to more than 81 percent in the case of Bulgarian exports (table 2.1). In

---

2. On the CMEA and its prospects, see Brabant (1989), Kenen (1991), and Schrenk (1990).

each of these countries, trade with the East is likely to fall, while trade with the West will rise. In this section we focus on the net effect of these two countervailing forces on openness, and we try to predict the long-run levels of EESU trade relative to national income.

Since it is expected that EESU will come to share features common to market-oriented countries in the long run, a rough first cut can be taken by projecting from the openness levels of comparator countries of similar size and structure and at similar levels of development. The problem is that it is not clear which countries should be taken as comparators. At one extreme are countries such as Germany, Finland, and Austria, which are close neighbors with a not-too-dissimilar cultural heritage but much higher levels of income. At the other extreme are a few upper-income developing countries such as South Korea and Taiwan. In the middle lie a group of Southern European countries: Greece, Portugal, and Spain. Table 2.2 presents statistics on merchandise exports–GNP ratios for EESU and for these potential comparators.

It is impossible to draw any clear-cut conclusions from these figures. Bulgaria appears to be fairly open by Western standards, whereas Poland, Yugoslavia, and the Soviet Union are not. Hungary and Romania compare favorably with Spain and Greece, but unfavorably with Austria, Finland, or Germany. Czechoslovakia is in the middle of the range. Remember, moreover, that national income figures for these countries are highly uncertain, and that the openness levels in EESU would have appeared much larger had we used the World Bank estimates for GNP (where available) rather than the PlanEcon estimates.

As the Soviet Union shows *in extremis*, it is difficult to assess levels of openness using comparator countries without making allowance for differences in size (as well as level of development). Larger countries will generally be more closed, everything else remaining the same (for example, US merchandise exports amounted to no more than 6.5 percent of GNP in 1988). Furthermore, there may be a nonlinear relationship between a country's level of development and its openness.

Therefore, we have undertaken a more systematic exercise which relies on the experience of a large group of nonsocialist countries. Using 1988 data on income levels, population, and a number of dummy variables, we have identified the "normal" relationship between such variables and openness on the basis of a regression across 91 countries.

TABLE 2.2   Eastern Europe and the Soviet Union: merchandise exports as a share of GNP, actual 1988 and predicted (percentages)

Country	Actual	Predicted[a] Current incomes	EC incomes
Bulgaria	34	23	26
Czechoslovakia	19	23	25
Hungary	15	23	26
Poland	7	19	22
Romania	13	19	24
Soviet Union	7	9	9[b]
Yugoslavia	11	20	23
Comparator countries			
Austria	26		
Finland	23		
West Germany	27		
South Korea	39		
Spain	13		
Portugal	28		
Greece	12		

a. The predicted ratios are based on a cross-country regression of merchandise exports–GNP ratios with 91 country observations. The independent variables used were GNP, logarithm of GNP, logarithm of population, and dummies for countries with export–GNP ratios greater than 40 percent, developed countries, Middle East, Latin America, and sub-Saharan Africa. Other independent variables (such as land area and f.o.b.–c.i.f. differentials) were consistently insignificant and altered the predicted ratios very little. The R-squared for the regression used is 0.79.

b. The regression predicts openness for the Soviet Union at the EC level of income to be 4 percent, which is lower than the current-incomes ratio. Since a reduction in openness is unlikely in our full catch-up scenario, we have kept the ratio constant at 9 percent.

Our statistical model has a reasonably good fit, explaining close to 80 percent of the variation in openness across countries. The parameters estimated in this way were then applied to data on income and population of EESU to derive predictions of openness. We tried different specifications, but predictions made with alternative combinations of right-hand-side variables proved remarkably close to each other. Table 2.2 contains the results. Two sets of predictions are reported: the first are based on current levels of income, whereas the second assume that EESU will attain the average EC level of income. We will focus on the first of these here.

These estimates are naturally subject to large margins of error.[3] Even allowing for this, however, the results suggest that openness in some of the countries of the region diverges substantially from the normal experience in nonsocialist countries. This is particularly true in the case of Poland and Yugoslavia, where predicted openness levels are roughly double their current levels. In Bulgaria, by contrast, the actual export share (34 percent) greatly exceeds the prediction of 23 percent. Not coincidentally, Bulgaria is also the country with the highest degree of reliance on CMEA trade (see table 2.1). At least in this one case, therefore, socialist trading arrangements appear, on balance, to have encouraged trade rather than discouraged it. Yugoslavia, on the other hand, was not a CMEA member, and Poland's intra–CMEA trade is the lowest among CMEA members. The other countries appear less open than they should be, but in most cases the differences are within margins of statistical error. Czechoslovakia and the Soviet Union are only slightly less open than the norm.

SOME SCENARIOS

We turn next to the implications for world trade. This entails combining our predicted levels of openness with levels of real income to generate dollar values of exports.

---

3. It is possible to have a sense of these errors by comparing the openness levels predicted by the model for the following countries with actual levels (in parentheses): Austria, 27 percent (26 percent); Finland, 29 percent (23 percent); Germany, 19 percent (27 percent); Italy, 19 percent (17 percent); Portugal, 21 percent (28 percent); Spain, 20 percent (13 percent). Although the range of prediction errors is large, the errors do not seem to be systematic. One can hope, therefore, that they balance out for EESU as a whole.

T A B L E 2.3   Eastern Europe and the Soviet Union: merchandise exports, actual 1988 and predicted

| | Actual | | Predicted[a] | | | |
| | | | Medium run[b] | | Full catch-up[c] | |
Country	Billions of dollars	As share of world exports	Billions of dollars	As share of world exports	Billions of dollars	As share of world exports
Bulgaria	17.3	0.64	11.7	0.42	31.4	0.98
Czechoslovakia	23.0	0.85	27.3	0.98	52.4	1.63
Hungary	10.0	0.37	15.8	0.57	37.0	1.15
Poland	14.0	0.52	39.3	1.42	112.2	3.48
Romania	12.6	0.47	18.0	0.65	74.1	2.30
Yugoslavia	12.8	0.48	23.1	0.83	72.8	2.26
Total EE6	89.7	3.33	135.2	4.88	379.9	11.80
Soviet Union	110.5	4.10	143.1	5.16	345.9	10.74
Total EESU	200.2	7.43	278.3	10.04	725.8	22.54

a. The figures for the dollar value of exports ignore the increase in EESU exports that would have taken place in the absence of integration into the world economy. Assuming that EESU and world exports would have otherwise grown at the same rate, the figures in the columns for the EESU share in world exports are insensitive to assumptions regarding the trend growth in world trade.

b. Income at current levels, with openness as predicted at current income levels.

c. Income at the EC average, with openness as predicted at that level of income.

We consider two alternative scenarios for real incomes in EESU and report the implications in table 2.3. At one extreme, our full catch-up scenario assumes that all countries in the region reach the same level of per capita income as the average for the European Community. As discussed above, this can be interpreted as an optimistic view of the long run. Alternatively, it can be interpreted as an upper limit to the likely magnitude of trade volume changes. This full catch-up scenario assumes quite rapid growth rates sustained over a long period. On average, the EE6 would need to grow by more than 8 percent per year for 20 years to attain this goal. (They would need to grow by 3 percent to 3.5 percent per year just to maintain their current income levels relative to the Community, and by an additional 5 percent per year in order to catch up to the average EC income level within two decades.)

The other scenario takes current income levels as given. This could be interpreted as a successful medium-run scenario (two to five years) in which trade restrictions are dismantled and market signals improve resource allocation, but in which the longer-run gains from growth have not yet materialized.

One could also envisage intermediate scenarios between these two cases. For example, it is possible that only Czechoslovakia, Hungary, and Poland will undertake the transition successfully. The implications of such a scenario can be read off table 2.3 by focusing only on the appropriate entries. Other scenarios can be constructed in a similar manner and are left to the reader's imagination.

The main message of table 2.3 is that EESU will make a major impact on global trade volumes only if the region's income rises appreciably. The impact of an increase in openness alone will be rather limited. Hence, if all of Eastern Europe and the Soviet Union became market economies overnight but remained at current income levels, our predictions imply that $78 billion per year in additional exports would be generated. The share of EESU in world trade would rise from 7.4 percent to 10.0 percent. This may not be an insignificant increase, but it is well within realistic expectations as to how much additional trade the world economy can accommodate.

The impact is much larger in the full catch-up scenario: the additional trade generated here would amount to $525.6 billion per year, and the region's share in world trade would triple to 22.5 percent. However, this transformation would take place gradually over many years, even in the best of circumstances. Suppose, for example, that it took 20 years for EESU to reach average per capita income levels of the European Community, and thus for EESU's exports to grow to 22.5 percent of world trade. That would imply an average increase in annual growth of world trade of just under 0.6 percent.

It may well be that the Soviet Union, Yugoslavia, Romania, and perhaps Bulgaria will be preoccupied mostly with internal matters rather than with external liberalization over the next few years. Removing these four countries leaves Czechoslovakia, Hungary, and Poland as the sources of trade expansion. These three countries taken together are expected to increase their share of world trade to 3.0 percent in the medium-run scenario (from 1.7 percent now), and to 6.3 percent in the full catch-up scenario. Poland, with the largest economy among the three, will account for most of this increase.

The primary determinant of the trade impact, therefore, will be the extent and speed of progress made in raising income levels. Even if such progress is widespread, the full effects will not be felt for some time. This does not imply, however, that the impact on specific markets (and particularly the European Community) will likewise be small. The next section suggests otherwise.

Direction of Trade

As mentioned above, the collapse of CMEA trading arangements and the growing influence of market forces in EESU is likely to lead to a reorientation of these countries' trade away from each other and toward Western markets. Since the intra–CMEA component of these countries' trade is very high (as shown in table 2.1), the potential for reallocation is also very large. What can we say about the likely trade pattern of these countries as liberalization proceeds?

There are two sorts of evidence one can use in addressing this question. The first draws on the experience of comparator countries, as was done in the previous section. The trade patterns of countries such as Austria, Finland, and Spain provide useful information on the direction that the Eastern European countries' trade will take, if the transition is successful. However, we also want to incorporate specific country characteristics in our predictions.

The second type of evidence is the pre–World War II experience of the Eastern European countries themselves. Before the war all of the countries of the region, except the Soviet Union, had market economies. Their trading patterns at that time presumably reflected some key underlying features—geographical proximity to markets, natural resource endowments, production complementarities, cultural similarities, and so on—which will be recovered as determinants of bilateral trade once these economies return to market principles.

COMPARISON WITH INTERWAR TRADE PATTERNS

In the following analysis, we will systematically combine both types of evidence to construct a predicted long-run trade matrix for the Eastern European countries. But first let us focus on the prewar trade relations of these countries. The initial problem we have is in selecting a benchmark year that reflects the natural tendencies of EESU trade, unencumbered by the effects of business cycles or special commercial restrictions. From this perspective, the 1930s are ruled out. Trade patterns of the 1930s were highly distorted as a result of the Great Depression and the growing bilateralism in commercial relations during that decade. In most of the countries of Central and Eastern Europe, trade volumes peaked in the late 1920s and then started to fall sharply (see figure 2.1). The Soviet Union was an exception, as it had been already fairly isolated from the world economy and was still recovering from the effects of its civil war (figure 2.2). Therefore, a year like 1928 would appear to be the latest "normal" year for the prewar period. And since we are lucky enough to have a world trade matrix for 1928 compiled by the League of Nations, we base our analysis on that year.

Table 2.4 displays direction-of-trade statistics for individual Eastern European countries and the Soviet Union for 1928, as well as the corresponding figures for 1989. Partners listed are the present-day European Community, the United States, Japan, the rest of Eastern Europe, and the Soviet Union; more detailed statistics on individual partners are reported in appendix A. The table also includes a column labeled

FIGURE 2.1 Czechoslovakia, Finland, Germany, and Hungary:
merchandise trade, 1923–38

1927 = 100

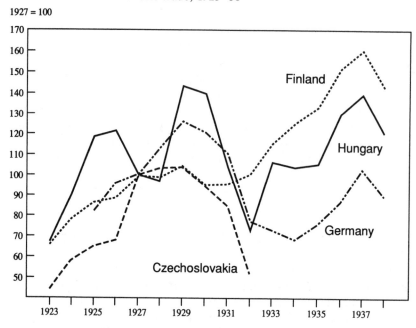

FIGURE 2.2 Soviet Union: merchandise trade, 1925–38

1927 = 100

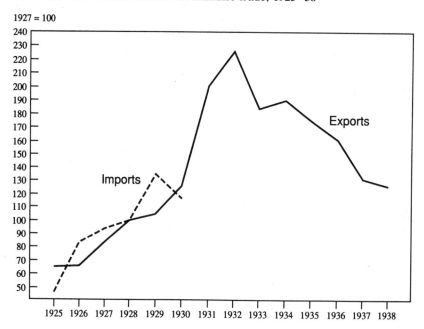

TABLE 2.4 Eastern Europe and the Soviet Union: geographical composition of trade, 1928, 1989, and predicted (percentages of total)[a]

Country and partner	Imports			Exports		
	1928	1989	Predicted	1928	1989	Predicted
Bulgaria						
EC	61.63	13.66	56.55	64.47	7.78	57.12
United States	2.33	1.54	2.64	1.32	0.87	3.27
Japan	0.00	1.39	3.93	0.00	0.59	1.55
Eastern Europe	20.93	11.53	8.67	11.84	17.40	7.83
Soviet Union	0.00	57.39	10.05	0.00	58.10	9.07
Other	15.12	14.48	18.15	22.37	15.26	21.15
Czechoslovakia						
EC	54.79	15.37	55.02	43.92	16.46	46.28
United States	5.94	0.32	3.48	5.56	0.56	4.73
Japan	0.07	0.33	3.95	0.19	0.76	1.55
Eastern Europe	16.67	16.66	7.69	20.55	16.45	10.77
Soviet Union	1.04	45.58	10.20	1.32	43.14	14.28
Other	21.49	21.74	19.66	28.46	22.64	22.40
Hungary						
EC	32.40	30.93	47.07	25.00	24.15	37.16
United States	3.63	1.60	2.78	0.82	2.83	2.77
Japan	0.00	1.21	3.72	0.00	1.15	1.40
Eastern Europe	40.22	14.25	12.47	33.61	14.41	15.03
Soviet Union	0.28	24.28	14.94	0.41	28.29	18.01
Other	23.46	27.74	19.02	40.16	29.17	25.62

Table continues next page

Country and partner	Imports			Exports		
	1928	1989	Predicted	1928	1989	Predicted
Poland						
EC	54.39	27.73	55.69	55.88	30.45	51.18
United States	13.95	1.78	5.43	0.84	2.73	2.94
Japan	0.00	1.41	3.99	0.29	0.97	1.59
Eastern Europe	9.09	13.46	6.00	16.60	14.13	9.31
Soviet Union	1.10	26.11	8.96	1.68	24.96	13.89
Other	21.47	29.50	19.93	24.71	26.77	21.09
Romania						
EC	50.15	7.75	53.04	53.85	17.54	49.98
United States	5.44	1.60	3.31	0.37	2.47	2.73
Japan	0.00	0.51	3.87	0.00	1.28	1.47
Eastern Europe	25.08	15.13	9.49	22.34	9.17	11.43
Soviet Union	0.60	36.04	11.59	0.00	30.41	13.96
Other	18.73	38.97	18.70	23.44	39.12	20.43
Yugoslavia						
EC	39.06	39.52	49.38	53.13	38.43	49.75
United States	5.15	5.14	3.17	1.04	5.13	2.99
Japan	0.00	1.48	3.78	0.00	0.26	1.47
Eastern Europe	30.47	11.20	10.49	20.83	10.08	10.86
Soviet Union	0.00	15.13	13.40	0.00	19.85	13.87
Other	25.32	27.54	19.77	25.00	26.26	21.05
Soviet Union						
EC	35.50	18.33	52.53	61.09	26.43	55.23
United States	19.61	5.71	6.94	3.86	1.27	4.26
Japan	0.33	4.10	4.17	1.37	4.82	2.09
Eastern Europe	3.25	36.88	11.10	2.43	36.73	13.90
Other	41.31	34.98	25.26	31.25	30.76	24.52

a. See text for methodology.

"predicted," which includes our estimates of posttransition trade shares. We will discuss these predictions below.

What is immediately evident in comparing the 1928 statistics with those for 1989 is the sharply reduced importance of the members of the present-day European Community in the trade of EESU, as well as the corresponding increase (for the Eastern European countries) in the importance of the Soviet Union. Note that for the EE6 (i.e., excluding the Soviet Union), the intratrade component in 1989 is not significantly higher than would have been expected from the interwar experience. In other words, there was substantial trade integration among the EE6 even prior to the formation of the CMEA. The CMEA appears mainly to have fostered trade with the Soviet Union: all the countries of the region have greatly increased their trade shares with the Soviet Union, which in turn has become much more dependent on the EE6. This increase in Soviet–EE6 trade mirrors the decline in EESU–EC trade.

Although suggestive, the 1928 composition of trade is far from being a reliable guide to future trade patterns. Even if we assume that the Eastern European countries will revert fully to the trading norms of nonsocialist countries, in the intervening years since 1928 these norms will have been altered by differential economic performance among the Western countries. Take, for example, Poland's trade with two of its partners, the United Kingdom and Japan. Before the war, the United Kingdom was Poland's third-largest trade partner (behind Germany and the United States on the import side, and behind Germany and Austria on the export side). Japan, by contrast, held an insignificantly small share of Poland's trade. The United Kingdom's position in the world economy has slipped considerably since the war, whereas Japan's has risen. In order to use the interwar data sensibly we have to make allowance for this shift. The United Kingdom will probably now occupy a less important role in Poland's trade than it did before the war, whereas Japan is likely to have a more important share. But once such adjustments are made, the prewar trade pattern can still provide useful information on the future composition of trade.[4]

---

4. There are other problems in drawing inferences from interwar trade patterns. For example, Poland's borders changed substantially after World War II, and Germany was split in two. Thus, some of Poland's 1928 trade originated in what is now part of the

COMBINING INTERWAR EVIDENCE WITH EVIDENCE FROM COMPARATOR COUNTRIES

To develop our projections, we combine evidence on the interwar trade patterns reported above with information on how the trade patterns of comparator countries have evolved since then. Underlying our approach is the assumption that, had the Eastern European countries not become socialist, they would have developed in a manner similar to that experienced by a group of comparator countries made up of Austria, Finland, Germany, Italy, Portugal, and Spain. Note that four of these countries are members of the European Community, although two of those four (Spain and Portugal) have joined only recently. Therefore, our scenario assumes that EESU will have access to EC markets at the "average" level exhibited by these comparators; later we will discuss the realism of this assumption. The analysis is based on a comparison of two trade matrices, one for 1928 and the other for 1989. On the basis of 1928 trade shares and a host of partner dummy variables, we estimated a statistical model that "predicts" the 1989 shares of 33 partners—26 Western partners plus the 7 countries of EESU—in the trade of these comparator countries. The inclusion of partner dummy variables allows us to control for differential growth in partner countries' trade potential since the war. (This is the adjustment needed in the example of Poland's trade with the United Kingdom and Japan, discussed above.) Our regressions provide quite respectable results: they explain more than 70 percent of the variation in the direction of trade for the comparator countries in 1989 (see appendix A).

We undertake two further adjustments before constructing a matrix of predicted trade shares. The observed 1989 trade between, say, Germany and France reflects a certain portion of trade that would not have taken place had the socialist countries remained in the international trading system. In the absence of the CMEA, France, Germany, and all the other Western countries presumably would have traded a bit more

---

Soviet Union, and likewise some of Germany's 1928 trade was generated in what is now part of Poland.

with the Eastern European countries and a bit less with each other. Therefore, predictions based on the observed 1989 trade shares of the Western countries are likely to overestimate the amount of trade that will now be diverted to Western markets. We adjust for this by estimating the reduction in trade with the socialist countries experienced by the comparator countries and scaling down the otherwise predicted trade shares by a corresponding factor.

Second, we adjust for the downward bias in our estimates for Soviet trade. In 1928, Soviet trade with the outside world was barely recovering from the effects of the October 1917 Revolution and the ensuing civil war. Even though the New Economic Policy then in force was considerably more liberal that what came before or after it, the Soviet Union's importance in the trade of our comparator countries stood in 1928 at an unnaturally low level. Estimates based on the 1928 trade matrix will therefore greatly underestimate the amount of trade that would take place with a healthy, market-oriented Soviet Union. Indeed, our estimated shares for trade with the Soviet Union came out very small. To adjust for this, we have assumed that the Soviet Union will occupy a position in trade proportional to that of intra–EE6 trade. The proportionality factor was in turn determined for each EE6 country individually, by taking the ratio of the global trade volume of the Soviet Union to that of the EE6 (excluding the country in question), as reported in our medium-run scenario in table 2.3. More details on our procedures are provided in appendix A.

Having estimated the parameters of our statistical model and adjusted them in the above manner, we use them to predict posttransition trade patterns for EESU on the basis of their own 1928 trade. The results are portrayed in the third and sixth columns of table 2.4. Details with respect to specific trade partners are reported in appendix tables A.3 through A.9.

We should stress the interpretation to be attached to our predicted trade shares. These represent our "best" estimate of the Eastern European countries' geographical composition of trade, under the dual assumptions that these countries had never become socialist and that their trade would have developed after 1928 in parallel with the "average" pattern exhibited by our comparator countries. Our estimates combine information on the EESU's 1928 trade pattern with the trends exhibited by the comparators' trade since then and adjust for the special position of the Soviet Union in 1928. However, the analysis ignores the possibility that EESU may have forged strong complementarities with each other during 45 years of socialist development—complementarities that will persist even in the absence of the CMEA and of socialist planning.

What these tables show most forcefully is that the predicted redirection of trade toward Western markets is large by any definition. In fact, it is often larger than would have been estimated on the basis of interwar trade patterns alone. Combined exports to the European Community, the United States, and Japan are predicted to rise to somewhere in the range of 40 percent to 62 percent of the Eastern European countries' total exports. This is a particularly sharp jump for those countries where the present combined share of these partners is extremely low, namely, Bulgaria (9 percent), Czechoslovakia (18 percent), and Romania (21 percent). But it represents a large increase even for Poland (from 34 percent) and Hungary (from 28 percent), where trade has been less concentrated on other CMEA members. These figures imply a correspondingly dramatic reduction in the bilateral trade of the EE6 (particularly Bulgaria, Czechoslovakia, and Romania) with the Soviet Union.

The European Community accounts for the bulk of the predicted reorientation toward the West. For most of EESU, the predicted trade share of the Community lies in the range of 45 percent to 55 percent. The predominance of the Community reflects not only the prewar trade patterns but also the fact that our comparator countries have become more integrated with member countries of the Community since then. That is true even though two countries in our comparator group (Austria and Finland) are not EC members.

When we turn to the breakdown of trade by specific partner (appendix tables A.3 through A.9), we find the predictable result that the largest absolute increases in trade shares almost always involve Germany.[5] Hence Germany will be the main beneficiary of the redirection of these countries' imports; it will also be the market that will have to absorb a

---

5. Note that prewar trade data are for a unified Germany whereas the 1989 data are for West Germany alone. So our predictions understate the trade that will take place with a unified Germany.

disproportionate share of their exports. France and Italy will play similar roles, but to a smaller extent than Germany. In general, only small increases (and in the case of Yugoslavia a decrease) in export shares to the United States are predicted. Not surprisingly, countries of the region are expected to experience relatively large increases in imports from Japan, but only small increases in exports there. Spain and the Netherlands are also predicted to play a substantially more important role in the trade of these countries than they have in the past.

Although the trade shares of the 26 Western partners are expected to increase almost across the board, there are some interesting declines. In the case of Poland, a redirection of trade away from Switzerland is projected. Romania's and Yugoslavia's trade with Iran and Iraq is predicted to fall (in relative terms). The trade shares of China are expected to decline in almost all of EESU.

IMPACT ON SPECIFIC MARKETS: SOME SCENARIOS

By assuming that EESU will develop and trade in a manner similar to the comparator countries, we have also implicitly assumed that they will have generally unhindered access to the markets of Western countries, and to those of the European Community in particular. But how plausible is this assumption in light of the major geographical reorientation our estimates point to?

To see what the implications would be, we now combine our predicted trade shares with the volume-of-trade effects discussed earlier to arrive at some estimates of the dollar value of potential new trade created in specific Western markets. As before, we consider alternative scenarios regarding the extent to which the transition succeeds. Our full catch-up scenario assumes that per capita incomes in all of EESU rise to the EC average. Our medium-run scenario assumes full liberalization but unchanged real income levels. For the purposes of these calculations, we assume that EESU will have balanced trade. But alternative scenarios can also be constructed by adjusting our import and export figures appropriately.

Tables 2.5 through 2.7 present estimated trade effects for the European Community, Germany alone, and the United States. Table 2.5

shows that EC trade with EESU currently accounts for around 4 percent to 5 percent of total EC trade (including intra–EC trade). In the medium run, liberalization (without income growth) would lead to a rise in this share to 12 percent. In the full catch-up scenario, EESU would account for more than a quarter of total EC trade. The total volume of EC–EESU trade is predicted to rise by around $100 billion per year in the medium run, and by more than $200 billion per year in the full catch-up scenario. These effects are split roughly equally between the Soviet Union and the EE6.

The long-run effects would naturally be spread out over a number of years. However, even the medium-run increase in trade indicated by these numbers is extremely large. This point can be seen even more starkly in the case of Germany (table 2.6). EESU are predicted to increase their share in Germany's trade to around 16 percent to 17 percent in the medium run, from 6 percent presently. The bilateral trade volume is estimated to grow by a factor of three or four, even in the absence of any output gains in EESU. The effect on the United States, by contrast, is much more modest (table 2.7): the share of EESU is estimated to rise from between 1 percent and 3 percent of US trade currently to no more than 3 percent to 4 percent in the medium run. Significantly, our estimates imply that US imports from EESU will expand rapidly, but that US exports will likely stagnate in the medium run. US exports to the region will not take off unless the region's income level rises considerably.

What should we make of these calculations? The most striking conclusion is the magnitude of the potential impact on the European Community. This impact is probably too large to be taken seriously as a realistic possibility. Although the Community has removed most quantitative restrictions on Eastern European imports, restrictions on farm products, textiles and clothing, and steel products remain. Czechoslovakia, Hungary, and Poland are presently negotiating association agreements with the Community, and the removal of these remaining restrictions is one of their top priorities. We think it is extremely unlikely that the Community will allow overall import penetration ratios to double or triple in the next few years, even if export volumes rise commensurately. Furthermore, since EESU exports will not increase uniformly across the board, actual import penetration ratios in specific

TABLE 2.5 European Community: shares of Eastern Europe and the Soviet Union in total trade, actual 1988 and predicted[a] (percentages)

Country	Actual		Medium run[b]		Full catch-up[c]	
	Imports	Exports	Imports	Exports	Imports	Exports
Bulgaria	0.13	0.23	0.56	0.55	1.27	1.24
Czechoslovakia	0.36	0.34	1.07	1.26	1.71	2.01
Hungary	0.23	0.30	0.50	0.62	0.97	1.22
Poland	0.41	0.38	1.70	1.84	4.06	4.37
Romania	0.21	0.09	0.76	0.80	2.62	2.75
Yugoslavia	0.47	0.49	0.97	0.96	2.56	2.52
Total EE6	1.80	1.83	5.57	6.03	13.20	14.12
Soviet Union	2.77	1.95	6.68	6.30	13.50	12.71
Total EESU	4.57	3.78	12.25	12.33	26.70	26.82
Memorandum: total EC trade with EESU (billions of dollars)	49.1	41.4	147.0	144.8	383.4	377.6

a. Assuming that the EESU share in EC trade would have remained unchanged in the absence of liberalization in EESU, these figures are insensitive to assumptions made regarding the trend growth in EC trade.

b. Income at current levels, with openness as predicted at current income levels.

c. Income at the EC average, with openness as predicted at that level of income.

Sources: Actual data from IMF, *Direction of Trade Statistics*, various issues, and World Bank (1990b).

T A B L E   2.6   Germany: shares of Eastern Europe and the Soviet Union in total trade, actual 1988 and predicted[a] (percentages)

Country	Actual		Medium run[b]		Full catch-up[c]	
	Imports	Exports	Imports	Exports	Imports	Exports
Bulgaria	0.16	0.36	0.72	0.68	1.54	1.43
Czechoslovakia	0.72	0.61	1.56	1.91	2.40	4.01
Hungary	0.47	0.57	0.62	0.85	1.15	2.23
Poland	0.76	0.56	2.61	2.47	5.96	7.45
Romania	0.26	0.12	1.00	1.06	3.28	4.72
Yugoslavia	0.63	0.70	0.95	1.18	2.38	4.09
Total EE6	3.01	2.92	7.45	8.15	16.71	23.93
Soviet Union	3.20	2.81	8.19	9.02	15.84	20.33
Total EESU	6.20	5.73	15.64	17.17	32.55	44.26
Memorandum: total German trade with EESU (billions of dollars)	15.4	18.5	60.4	54.6	156.4	142.2

a. Assuming that the EESU share in German trade would have remained unchanged in the absence of liberalization in EESU, these figures are insensitive to assumptions made regarding the trend growth in German trade.

b. Income at current levels, with openness as predicted at current income levels.

c. Income at the EC average, with openness as predicted at that level of income.

Sources: Actual data from IMF, *Direction of Trade Statistics,* various issues, and World Bank (1990b).

TABLE 2.7 United States: shares of Eastern Europe and the Soviet Union in total trade, actual 1988 and predicted[a] (percentages)

Country	Actual		Medium run[b]		Full catch-up[c]	
	Imports	Exports	Imports	Exports	Imports	Exports
Bulgaria	0.02	0.06	0.09	0.07	0.24	0.19
Czechoslovakia	0.04	0.03	0.31	0.23	0.58	0.43
Hungary	0.10	0.08	0.11	0.11	0.24	0.24
Poland	0.23	0.22	0.28	0.52	0.77	1.41
Romania	0.10	0.09	0.12	0.15	0.47	0.57
Yugoslavia	0.26	0.37	0.17	0.18	0.52	0.54
Total EE6	0.74	0.85	1.09	1.27	2.83	3.37
Soviet Union	0.41	2.59	1.51	2.42	3.51	5.54
Total EESU	1.15	3.44	2.60	3.69	6.34	8.92
Memorandum: total US trade with EESU (billions of dollars)	5.3	10.9	15.0	10.6	38.4	26.9

a. Assuming that the EESU share in US trade would have remained unchanged in the absence of liberalization in EESU, these figures are insensitive to assumptions made regarding the trend growth in US trade.

b. Income at current levels, with openness as predicted at current income levels.

c. Income at the EC average, with openness as predicted at that level of income.

Sources: Actual data from IMF, Direction of Trade Statistics, various issues, and World Bank (1990b).

"sensitive" sectors will have to be even larger. The more likely outcome is that the Community will build safeguards against import surges of this kind into any future relationship that it enters with the countries of Eastern Europe and the Soviet Union. In other words, serious trade restrictions will remain (as in agriculture and clothing) and possibly multiply. Also, some shifting of the burden onto third countries—those without strong EC affiliation or diplomatic clout—would also seem inevitable. At least some of the increase in EC imports from EESU will have to come at the expense of the exports of middle-income countries outside Europe.

As mentioned above, our estimates ignore one factor that will certainly limit the reorientation toward European markets: more than four decades of intra–CMEA specialization has surely created some production complementarities among the Eastern European countries that our statistical model does not account for. Trade based on such complementarities will go on at least until installed capital is thoroughly amortized. On the other hand, if the Soviet economy fails to recover, the EE6 will orient themselves toward the West even more. Since the European Community will be at the receiving end of any collapse in intra–EESU trade, it would appear to be in the interest of the Community to contribute to the recovery of the Soviet economy through financial and technical assistance.

Product Composition of Trade

So far the discussion has focused on the overall volume and direction of EESU trade. We now turn to the trends likely to emerge in the product composition of this trade.

Probably the best indicator we have of EESU's comparative advantage pattern is that reflected in its current trade with the West. There can be little doubt that this trade has been greatly distorted by centralized planning in the socialist countries and by misguided domestic pricing policies. This introduces a note of caution into any projection based on current trade patterns. Nonetheless, EESU's trade with the West was probably less distorted than intra–CMEA trade and may still be reflective of these countries' underlying pattern of comparative advantage.

A second note of caution has to do with the likely expansion in the overall volume of these countries' trade, as discussed above. Even if current trade flows with the West are a good guide to current comparative advantage, the future trade pattern is unlikely to be a simple radial blow-up of today's. All historical episodes of significant trade expansion have involved a great deal of product diversification in exports. Agricultural products, in particular, which may loom large in the exports of some of the Eastern European countries initially, could well be replaced in the longer run by manufactured products of increasing sophistication as their industrial sectors are rehabilitated.

With these caveats in mind, let us turn to the comparative advantage patterns reflected in current East-West trade flows. Table 2.8 shows an index of revealed comparative advantage for each of several broad trade categories constructed for the EE6 countries as a group and for the Soviet Union separately.[6] A positive number in the last two columns of the table indicates the presence of comparative advantage, and a negative number comparative disadvantage. The larger the number (in absolute value), the more significant is the implied comparative advantage or disadvantage.

The numbers indicate that the Soviet Union has a much more sharply differentiated pattern of comparative advantage than the Eastern European countries taken together. The Soviet Union has a strong revealed comparative advantage in crude materials (i.e., minerals) and fuels and a strong revealed comparative disadvantage in everything else, especially food, machinery, and miscellaneous manufacturing. The Soviet Union exhibits a significant comparative disadvantage in manufacturing as a whole. For the other countries the pattern is more mixed and less stark. The Eastern European countries appear to have a strong comparative advantage vis-à-vis the West in fuels, even though in intra–CMEA trade they are large net importers of fuels from the Soviet Union. Other product categories in which these countries have a revealed comparative advantage are food, crude materials, basic manu-

---

6. For a similar exercise involving four individual Eastern European countries (Czechoslovakia, Hungary, Poland, and Yugoslavia), see Fieleke (1990).

TABLE 2.8 **Eastern Europe and the Soviet Union: product composition of trade with the West and revealed comparative advantage, 1988** (billions of dollars except where indicated)

Product category	Exports to West		Imports from West		Revealed comparative advantage index[a]	
	Eastern Europe	Soviet Union	Eastern Europe	Soviet Union	Eastern Europe	Soviet Union
Primary products	5.7	4.0	3.7	5.1	0.17	-0.09
Food	3.2	0.5	1.9	4.2	0.21	-0.77
Crude materials	2.2	3.5	1.5	0.7	0.14	0.68
Fuels	3.4	14.6	0.5	0.2	0.72	0.97
Manufactures	17.6	6.1	20.0	20.8	-0.11	-0.52
Chemicals	3.2	1.5	4.4	3.1	-0.20	-0.32
Basic manufactures	6.6	3.3	4.9	6.6	0.10	-0.31
Machinery	3.4	1.1	8.6	9.0	-0.46	-0.77
Miscellaneous manufactures	4.3	0.2	2.0	2.1	0.32	-0.82
Total	26.8	24.8	24.3	26.3		

a. The index of revealed comparative advantage is calculated as $(X - \alpha M)/(X + \alpha M)$ for each product category, where α is an adjustment coefficient for unbalanced trade ($\alpha = 1.10$ and 0.94 for Eastern Europe and the Soviet Union, respectively).

Source: Calculated from Economic Commission for Europe (1989), table 2.23.

facturing, and miscellaneous manufacturing. They have a revealed comparative disadvantage in chemicals and machinery (which includes transport equipment).

Thus, although the Eastern European countries are net importers of manufactures taken as a whole, these numbers show that they are likely to have comparative advantage in many standardized, low-skill items in the basic and miscellaneous manufactures categories. In this respect, they are much like middle-income developing countries. The Soviet Union, on the other hand, is unlikely to export a considerable amount of manufactures; it will continue to trade energy and minerals for manufactured products.

The trade of EESU will no doubt continue to be influenced by current patterns of resource allocation within the region, at least in the short run. As distorted as these patterns may be, they are unlikely to disappear overnight, no matter how quickly the transition to markets takes place. Therefore, it is instructive also to take a look at current patterns of production, and to identify commodities that are abundant relative to local demand. Such commodities are likely to be sold cheaply in world markets and raise concerns about "dumping" in recipient markets. In fact, this appears to be happening already with respect to some of the agricultural and processed food exports of Poland and Hungary into the European Community.

Table 2.9 displays per capita agricultural production in EESU as a ratio of the world average for each of a number of commodities. Romania and Hungary are seen to be significant producers of cereals in per capita terms, even at current, presumably depressed levels of production. These two countries, together with Bulgaria, also produce significant quantities of sunflowers. Poland produces 27 times the world per capita average of rye; Czechoslovakia and the Soviet Union produce five to six times the world per capita average of barley. Hungary is a significant producer of meat, and Czechoslovakia and Poland of milk. In the area of processed foods, Hungary, Poland, Czechoslovakia, and Bulgaria would seem to have great potential in canned meat, fruit, and vegetables. These numbers bring out the potential of these countries to wreak havoc with the European Community's Common Agricultural Policy—a potential that would be magnified if improved incentives and pricing were to lead to gains in agricultural productivity.

TABLE 2.9   Eastern Europe and the Soviet Union: ratios of per capita agricultural production to world per capita production, average 1985–87

Product	Bulgaria	Czecho-slovakia	Hungary	Poland	Romania	Soviet Union	Yugo-slavia
Cereals, total	2.0	1.9	3.5	1.7	3.1	1.8	1.8
Wheat	3.9	3.4	5.2	1.8	2.6	2.7	1.9
Rye	0.8	5.1	2.4	27.2	0.3	8.2	0.4
Rice, paddy	0.1	n.a.	0.0	n.a.	0.1	0.1	0.0
Corn	2.2	0.7	6.6	0.0	7.8	0.5	4.4
Barley	3.0	6.0	2.2	3.0	2.6	4.9	0.7
Sorghum	n.a.	n.a.	0.1	n.a.	0.0	0.0	0.0
Millet	n.a.	0.0	0.2	n.a.	n.a.	1.8	0.0
Soybeans	0.3	n.a.	0.3	n.a.	0.8	0.1	0.3
Rapeseed	n.a.	4.6	2.3	7.3	0.4	0.1	1.1
Cottonseed	0.2	n.a.	n.a.	n.a.	n.a.	2.5	n.a.
Peanuts	0.1	n.a.	n.a.	n.a.	n.a.	0.0	n.a.
Sunflowers	11.6	0.8	17.3	n.a.	9.4	4.6	3.9
Roots and tubers	0.4	1.8	1.0	8.0	2.9	2.3	0.8
Pulses	0.8	1.3	2.1	1.1	1.3	2.8	0.8
Cotton lint	0.1	n.a.	n.a.	n.a.	n.a.	0.9	n.a
Meat	2.5	3.0	4.6	2.2	2.5	1.9	2.0
Milk	2.6	4.1	2.4	3.9	1.8	3.2	1.9
Eggs	2.7	2.0	3.4	1.8	2.9	2.4	1.5
Wool, greasy	4.1	0.4	1.1	0.5	2.2	1.8	0.5
Beef and veal, fresh	1.38	2.58	1.19	1.90	1.02	2.85	1.32

Mutton and lamb, fresh	4.83	0.45	0.26	0.43	1.65	1.71	1.50
Pork, fresh	3.14	4.17	7.41	3.50	2.97	1.68	2.69
Poultry, fresh	2.51	1.88	5.82	1.15	2.47	1.40	1.88
Meat, canned	15.00	5.62	15.25	6.37	n.a.	3.02	7.40
Hides	1.71	2.76	0.89	1.49	1.11	2.04	1.21
Skins	11.81	0.36	0.00	0.37	1.34	1.32	0.48
Butter	1.85	6.04	1.95	4.42	1.04	3.89	0.20
Cheese	7.08	4.76	2.89	4.10	1.39	2.30	1.98
Fruits, frozen	4.95	8.95	16.87	22.59	n.a.	n.a.	9.48
Fruits, canned	7.80	2.68	9.26	1.07	8.07	2.13	4.85
Vegetables, frozen	0.88	1.72	5.50	1.97	n.a.	0.01	1.40
Vegetables, canned	14.61	4.70	15.80	2.67	8.53	4.59	3.49
Fish, frozen	3.09	n.a.	0.20	1.86	1.81	4.28	0.02
Fish, canned	1.87	0.36	0.01	1.18	1.20	4.98	1.80
Sugar, raw	2.44	0.64	2.27	2.38	1.11	1.47	n.a.
Sugar, refined	3.20	3.97	2.91	3.06	1.95	3.32	2.57
Wine	6.48	1.34	2.62	1.03	5.23	0.77	1.93
Beer	3.26	6.71	4.01	1.48	2.18	0.84	2.42
Cigarettes	9.47	1.53	2.36	2.46	1.19	1.25	2.26

n.a. = not available.

Source: US Department of Agriculture, World Agriculture Trends and Indicators; United Nations (1987).

Table 2.10 undertakes the same exercise for a wide range of industrial products. In terms of crude materials, all the countries of the region appear to be important producers of coal, except for the Soviet Union, which is strong in crude oil, natural gas, and iron ore. In clothing and footwear, Poland and Czechoslovakia in particular appear very well positioned. In glass products, production is extremely high in relative per capita terms in all countries of the region except for Yugoslavia and the Soviet Union. Romania, Poland, and Czechoslovakia are strong in steel products, Bulgaria and Czechoslovakia in milling machines, Yugoslavia and Bulgaria in typewriters, Czechoslovakia and Romania in locomotives, Hungary in buses, and so on.

To summarize, the countries of Eastern Europe are likely to export agricultural goods, processed food, and a wide range of manufactured products, while remaining net importers of manufactures as a whole. The Soviet Union will basically export energy and crude materials. EESU as a whole will import machinery, chemicals, and other manufactured products. The numbers suggest that potentially disruptive EESU export surpluses in agriculture may well develop, especially if, as expected, the region experiences substantial productivity increases in agriculture.[7] As discussed above, these countries will expand trade mainly with the European Community. Hence, it may prove difficult for the Community's Common Agricultural Policy, already under assault in the General Agreement on Tariffs and Trade, to survive these changes. There is also potential for trouble in many of the industrial subsectors listed above.

The region's prospective trade pattern will involve a certain asymmetry with regard to the burden of adjustment borne by other countries. The increased Eastern European demand for capital and intermediate goods will benefit primarily the advanced industrial countries, which can supply these products. Eastern European exports, on the other

---

7. On this point see also CEPR (1990, 14–19), which provides a useful discussion of the agricultural potential of the region. The authors of this report calculate that a worldwide reduction in prices of around 10 percent may be needed to accommodate prospective EESU surpluses in grains. As the report notes, Western governments are unlikely to pass on such decreases to their producers.

hand, will compete with and displace the exports of the middle-income developing countries and perhaps also the Southern European countries. The middle-income countries are therefore likely to experience losses in market shares and a deterioration in their terms of trade while the richer countries experience an improvement.

The recent CEPR (1990) report is more optimistic about the impact on the developing countries. According to the authors of this report, the Eastern European countries are likely to develop a comparative advantage in goods that are intensive in human capital and skills, as the levels of educational attainment and scientific and technological mastery in these countries are high on average. The report provides a wide range of statistics on the education and composition of the Eastern European work force to underscore this point, concluding that, "These factor abundances suggest that among manufactures it is hi-tech goods rather than labour-intensive goods that represent Eastern Europe's area of comparative advantage" (CEPR 1990, 12). If indeed this turns out to be the case, EESU exports need not compete head-on with the labor-intensive exports of the developing countries.

While this is a plausible scenario, we think its likelihood depends critically on a number of factors, including the level of capital flows into the region; how foreign investors evaluate the labor skills potential of the region; and the exchange rates at which these countries integrate themselves into the world economy. We can imagine that if considerable capital flows are made available, these countries will be able to maintain relatively expensive currencies that overvalue their labor costs in dollar terms. That would undercut the incentive to compete in export markets on the basis of cheap labor. At the same time, large capital inflows attracted in part by the skills potential of the region would "validate" and unlock domestic human capital and set the stage for exports of relatively sophisticated, skill-intensive manufactures—especially if those flows came hand in hand with transfers of technology. Within ten years, Eastern Europe could look like Central or Western Europe rather than Southern Europe.

On the other hand, if capital is not so freely available, the prospects will look very different. EESU would not have the luxury of running large current account deficits with the West. Currencies would be undervalued and domestic labor costs cheap in dollar terms. The export expansion required early on would be based on labor-cost advantages

TABLE 2.10 Eastern Europe and the Soviet Union: ratios of per capita industrial production to world per capita production, 1985–87 average

Product	Bulgaria	Czecho-slovakia	Hungary	Poland	Romania	Soviet Union	Yugo-slavia
Hard coal	0.03	2.34	0.32	7.26	0.54	2.59	0.02
Brown coal	16.01	25.26	7.58	7.60	6.58	2.22	11.86
Crude petroleum	0.05	0.02	0.31	0.01	0.76	3.73	0.28
Natural gas	0.04	0.12	1.58	0.30	4.81	6.32	0.27
Iron ore	0.53	0.27	0.00	0.00	0.22	4.16	0.65
Yarn, wool	9.61	7.48	1.98	4.40	6.96	3.16	4.81
Yarn, cotton	3.08	2.93	1.86	1.65	2.36	1.90	1.88
Fabric, cotton	2.57	2.71	1.78	1.37	2.00	1.98	1.01
Fabric, wool	10.01	7.38	2.35	5.41	8.23	4.08	6.09
Trousers, men's and boys'	n.a.	n.a.	3.24	n.a.	n.a.	n.a.	4.27
Blouses, women's and girls'	n.a.	n.a.	1.58	n.a.	n.a.	n.a.	2.52
Leather, light	6.46	11.47	7.49	5.97	n.a.	2.82	5.14
Footwear (except rubber)	3.89	8.72	4.76	4.57	5.92	3.24	4.52
Footwear, other	n.a.	18.20	3.60	10.70	n.a.	n.a.	4.99
Sawn wood, coniferous	1.42	3.46	0.51	1.80	0.90	3.94	1.28
Sawnwood, broadleaf	1.35	1.99	2.89	0.82	4.63	1.72	3.67
Plywood	0.51	1.27	0.16	0.41	0.93	0.78	0.56
Newsprint	n.a.	0.65	n.a.	0.28	0.61	0.91	0.25
Paper, other	0.71	0.76	1.28	0.64	0.50	0.38	1.12
Paper, kraft	n.a.	2.50	1.33	0.78	1.23	n.a.	0.86
Hydrochloric acid	4.25	2.30	1.45	0.85	8.91	n.a.	2.48
Sulfuric acid	2.65	2.80	1.93	2.88	2.55	3.46	2.35

Product							
Caustic soda	1.54	2.83	2.34	1.50	4.73	1.54	1.08
Fertilizers, nitrogen	4.83	1.97	3.52	2.20	5.30	2.98	1.92
Fertilizers, phosphate	1.49	1.86	3.01	2.61	3.74	3.57	2.81
Insecticides, fungicides, herbicides, and disinfectants	2.82	2.00	12.52	1.84	3.07	1.97	4.07
Polypropylene	n.a.	7.26	6.27	1.07	n.a.	0.22	0.77
Soap	1.66	1.14	0.89	1.00	n.a.	2.69	0.59
Jet fuel	n.a.	n.a.	n.a.	n.a.	n.a.	n.a.	0.50
Motor gasoline	1.32	0.65	0.83	0.49	1.59	1.90	0.66
Tires, motor vehicle	1.24	1.87	0.38	0.96	1.37	1.43	3.00
Glass, drawn or blown	10.48	9.57	5.90	8.19	14.77	4.11	3.38
Bricks, clay	1.17	1.27	1.75	0.30	n.a.	0.98	1.43
Cement	2.77	3.01	1.77	1.93	2.46	2.19	1.73
Steel, crude, castings	n.a.	n.a.	2.72	6.13	12.63	n.a.	0.86
Steel, crude, ingots	2.36	6.88	2.24	2.88	4.21	3.96	0.56
Aluminum, unwrought	n.a.	0.94	1.78	0.28	2.66	2.34	2.66
Lead, unwrought	11.36	1.52	0.00	2.17	1.72	2.51	4.39
Zinc, unwrought	6.71	0.05	n.a.	3.20	1.52	2.44	3.45
Tin, unwrought	n.a.	0.98	n.a.	n.a.	n.a.	0.14	n.a.
Nails, etc.	5.90	9.73	6.43	5.48	n.a.	n.a.	4.87
Tractors (10 hp or more, except industrial and road)	0.99	4.22	0.04	2.93	3.05	3.72	0.01
Milling machines	12.23	12.39	0.33	3.25	n.a.	n.a.	4.91
Metal working presses	n.a.	6.89	n.a.	0.29	n.a.	n.a.	6.07
Bulldozers	2.44	n.a.	n.a.	n.a.	n.a.	8.46	1.45

TABLE 2.10 Eastern Europe and the Soviet Union (continued)

Product	Bulgaria	Czecho-slovakia	Hungary	Poland	Romania	Soviet Union	Yugo-slavia
Typewriters	8.69	3.09	0.00	0.98	n.a.	n.a.	7.98
Stoves, household	2.18	1.65	1.46	1.48	n.a.	n.a.	1.89
Sewing machines	n.a.	n.a.	0.10	3.15	0.46	1.49	1.73
Refrigerators, household	1.20	3.27	4.22	1.30	1.77	2.04	3.05
Washing machines, household	2.07	3.19	4.11	2.23	1.14	2.19	2.74
Televisions	1.03	1.51	1.95	0.80	0.98	1.48	1.17
Radios	0.20	0.41	0.30	2.41	0.86	0.92	0.27
Telephones	10.07	n.a.	1.24	3.81	n.a.	n.a.	1.08
Vacuum cleaners	n.a.	5.70	0.37	3.66	0.97	2.11	2.93
Locomotives, electric	n.a.	14.71	3.49	5.89	n.a.	3.68	0.99
Locomotives, diesel	n.a.	45.28	0.89	1.11	9.34	6.33	0.40
Rail passenger cars	n.a.	4.15	0.00	4.13	7.16	n.a.	1.20
Cars, passenger	0.32	1.60	n.a.	1.12	0.81	0.68	1.35
Buses and motor coaches	4.89	3.92	19.85	4.31	n.a.	0.97	2.92
Bicycles	0.57	2.64	1.28	2.09	n.a.	1.07	1.78
Cameras	n.a.	0.04	n.a.	0.00	n.a.	0.77	n.a.
Watches	0.00	0.13	n.a.	0.00	n.a.	1.29	0.00

n.a. = not available.
Source: United Nations (1987).

rather than on an abundance of human skills. In the absence of large-scale inflows of physical capital, and the associated transfer of technology, it is doubtful that the area's human capital can be transformed into a source of comparative advantage for exports of high-technology goods.

Current evidence suggests that the second scenario is the more likely one. For one thing, since 1989 the countries of the region have been more likely to err on the side of undervaluing their currencies. They are not running large trade deficits with the West; if anything, they are doing the opposite. Both Poland and Hungary have sizable trade surpluses in their trade with the West. Moreover, as we will discuss in the next chapter, large-scale capital inflows are unlikely to materialize anytime soon. Finally, the results of our survey of private investors, reported in the next chapter (and Appendix C), indicate that the high skill level of the labor force in the region is not perceived as a major attraction. Therefore, the inflow of private capital and technology needed to unlock the human capital potential of the region will be limited in scale. For all these reasons we believe that Eastern Europe is likely to make its entrance into the world economy, at least where manufactures are concerned, mainly as a low-cost producer of relatively standardized commodities rather than as a producer of human capital–intensive products.

Recent Developments in Polish and Hungarian Trade

The analyses reported above provide broad order-of-magnitude estimates of the potential impact of EESU transformation on world trade flows. The estimates for trade expansion with Western Europe are quite large—even when confined to those for Poland, Hungary, and Czechoslovakia alone. Thus, it is important to have a sense of the speed with which economic transformation in the region is likely to take place, and the speed with which the impact will be felt on trade flows. Here we briefly discuss the very recent trade experience of two countries as possible leading indicators: Poland, where the transformation to a market economy has been very rapid, and Hungary, where despite a more cautious approach considerable progress has been achieved.

POLAND

On 1 January 1990, Poland opened its economy to foreign trade virtually overnight. All import licenses were eliminated, trade was demonopolized, and almost all quantitative restrictions were removed. The only remaining form of trade restriction is tariffs, which average only around 8 percent. Similarly, there now exist no export controls on trade with the convertible-currency area. The zloty was devalued and made convertible for current account transactions. These measures went alongside a big-bang liberalization and stabilization package on the domestic side, aimed at bringing inflation down.

The trade figures for 1990 are somewhat distorted by the severe recession that followed the stabilization measures. Hence imports have taken a large dive, reflecting the collapse of industrial production at home, but exports to the convertible-currency area increased by 20 percent in the first seven months of 1990 (table 2.11) and have risen further since then. The increase was particularly marked in minerals, chemicals, and agricultural products. Specific items such as shoes, potatoes, and steel pipes have made major gains. This sharp rise in exports no doubt reflects in part the scramble for foreign markets caused by the recession at home. But it also reflects the effects of domestic liberalization, devaluation, and the collapse of the CMEA and of Soviet trade. What is particularly important from our standpoint is the speed of the supply response. The Polish experience shows that a radical and credible program is capable of bringing forth a large increase in exports in a matter of months.[8]

Table 2.11 shows the differential trade response for Western and Eastern markets. Polish exports to the developed West increased by 22 percent from January to July 1990 while ruble exports to EESU fell by 3 percent. The import response has been asymmetric also. Imports from the developed West fell by 28 percent while ruble imports from the East fell by 40 percent. The net effect is that the share of the advanced

---

8. Similar responses have been observed in liberalization episodes in the developing world, for example in Korea in the mid-1960's, Chile in the mid-1970's, Turkey in the mid-1980's, and Mexico since 1985.

TABLE 2.11 Poland: composition of trade during the first seven months of 1989 and 1990[a] (millions of dollars except where noted)

Category	Exports (f.o.b.)					Imports (f.o.b.)					Trade balance	
	1-7 1989	1-7 1990	Value	Price	Quantity	1-7 1989	1-7 1990	Value	Price	Quantity	1-7 1989	1-7 1990
			Percentage growth in					Percentage growth in				
Convertible-currency trade	4,757	5,578	17.3	-2.2	19.9	4,390	3,101	-29.4	-1.3	-28.4	368	2,477
Nonsocialist countries	4,270	4,872	14.1	-2.6	17.2	3,909	2,630	-32.7	-3.6	-30.2	361	2,242
Developed West	3,454	4,197	21.5	n.a.	n.a.	3,395	2,440	-28.1	n.a.	n.a.	59	1,757
Developing countries	816	676	-17.2	n.a.	n.a.	514	189	-63.2	n.a.	n.a.	302	487
Socialist countries	487	706	44.9	0.9	43.6	481	471	-2.1	13.6	-13.8	7	235
Nonconvertible currency trade (millions of rubles)	6,349	6,174	-2.8	5.7	-8.0	5,807	3,482	-40.0	-5.4	-36.6	543	2,692
Soviet Union	3,823	3,541	-7.4	n.a.	n.a.	3,238	1,996	-38.4	n.a.	n.a.	586	1,545
Other socialist countries	2,526	2,633	4.2	n.a.	n.a.	2,569	1,486	-42.2	n.a.	n.a.	-43	1,147
Nonsocialist trade, total	4,270	4,872	14.1	-2.6	17.2	3,909	2,630	-32.7	-3.6	-30.2	360	2,242
Fuel and energy	546	591	8.3	4.9	3.3	238	159	-33.2	1.3	-34.1	308	432
Metals	677	832	22.8	-10.2	36.8	314	203	-35.5	-2.4	-33.9	363	629
Machinery	931	918	-1.4	2.5	-3.9	1,053	1,320	25.3	2.4	22.4	-122	-402
Chemicals	455	638	40.1	-12.7	60.4	820	384	-53.2	-3.2	-51.6	-364	254
Food	628	640	1.9	-3.7	5.9	497	213	-57.2	0.0	-57.2	130	427
Agriculture	251	330	31.5	-5.9	39.8	537	49	-90.8	18.7	-92.3	-286	281
Other[b]	782	924	18.2	n.a.	n.a.	449	302	-32.7	n.a.	n.a.	332	621

n.a. = not available.

a. Data for both years are for January through July only.

b. This category includes minerals, wood and paper, light industry, construction, and forestry.

Source: Reprinted with permission from PlanEcon Report.

industrial countries in Polish exports increased from 46 percent to 61 percent in the first seven months of 1990 alone, while the corresponding share of EESU went from 44 percent to 30 percent.

A similar transformation has taken place on the import side. Germany has now replaced the Soviet Union as Poland's most important trade partner. To some extent these numbers reflect the present disarray in the Soviet Union. But they also show that a very rapid redirection of trade is possible once the rules of the game change. That is, the numbers discussed in the previous sections could easily become a reality within a couple of years if the countries of the region make a concerted commitment to liberalization.

HUNGARY

In Hungary, where the domestic economy has been more stable than was Poland's at the time of its opening, the government has been pursuing a gradual program of trade liberalization, with support from the World Bank and the IMF. Since 1989, domestic consumer prices have been progressively liberalized, and import licensing requirements have been eliminated for an increasing number of commodities. By January 1991 only 10 percent of imports remained on the restricted list. Although the trade and payments regime remains generally more restrictive than in Poland, the trend toward opening up is unmistakable. As a consequence of this, as well as of the problems being experienced in Soviet trade, Hungary's trade (table 2.12) displays some of the same trends as Poland's.

Compared with 1989, Hungary's dollar trade with the industrial countries increased substantially in 1990, while its trade with the socialist countries fell by an almost identical proportion. On the export side, total exports to the industrial countries increased in dollar terms by 23.5 percent, and exports to the European Community increased by an even higher 27.4 percent. There was a particularly dramatic rise in exports to (West) Germany, amounting to almost 50 percent (not shown in the table). Germany has now become as important a trade partner for Hungary as the Soviet Union, even if one excludes trade with the former East Germany. Ruble exports to the socialist countries,

TABLE 2.12 Hungary: composition of trade, 1989 and 1990 (millions of dollars except where noted)

Category	Exports			Imports		
	1989	1990	Percentage growth	1989	1990	Percentage growth
Convertible-currency trade						
Socialist countries	557.4	638.0	14.5	501.3	476.9	-4.9
Industrial West	4,835.5	5,972.1	23.5	4,574.8	5,294.8	15.7
of which: EC	2 711.2	3,455.3	27.4	2,634.3	2,905.5	10.3
Developing countries	715.5	678.3	-5.2	478.3	593.2	24.0
Fuels and energy	215.3	235.6	9.4	43.0	537.5	1,150.0
Raw materials	2,712.0	3,241.6	19.5	3,315.6	3,249.1	-2.0
Machinery, transport equipment, capital goods	627.6	830.9	32.4	948.9	1,132.5	19.3
Consumer goods	901.1	1,114.9	23.7	641.8	816.9	27.3
Food	1,652.4	1,865.5	12.9	605.0	628.9	4.0
Nonconvertible currency trade (millions of rubles)						
Socialist countries	7,645.9	5,840.7	-23.6	7,124.3	5,938.3	-16.6
Industrial West	31.3	97.3	210.9	6.0	0.0	-100.0
Developing countries	4.2	1.8	-57.1	1.3	1.1	-15.4

Source: Preliminary data from the Central Statistical Office, Budapest.

meanwhile, fell by 23.6 percent. There was a similar, if somewhat less marked, reorientation on the import side as well. With respect to product composition, export growth has been particularly strong in raw materials, capital goods, and consumer goods, while imports have expanded predominantly in consumer goods and capital goods (table 2.12).

Hence, the experience in both countries shows that the spillover effects of the dual shocks of domestic liberalization and collapse of the CMEA will be felt rapidly. The countries of the region have the capacity to reorient their trade to the West very quickly indeed. However, these spillovers will probably be limited over the next couple of years to the trade of Poland, Hungary, and Czechoslovakia.

Conclusions

We have presented in this chapter a number of scenarios and quantitative implications with respect to the impact of Eastern Europe and the Soviet Union on world trade. It is appropriate to end on a cautionary note. There is a great range of uncertainty with respect to the likely developments in each of the countries of the region, and in the Soviet Union in particular. The numbers we have presented are likely to end up wide of the mark. But we think they are useful nonetheless in helping frame the issues and focus thinking on the potential impact. We end this chapter by summarizing our main conclusions.

With the possible exceptions of Poland and Yugoslavia, substantial increases in the openness of the countries of the region are unlikely. Therefore, the overall trade volumes of EESU will expand primarily as a result of a rise in living standards and output levels. However, because any increase in income will take time, the global trade impact will be spread out over a number of years. Moreover, macroeconomic and political developments may well force some countries in the region to move away from further openness. Foreign-exchange shortages (due to adverse terms-of-trade developments), macroeconomic instability, and domestic political turmoil could push some of the governments to turn inward rather than outward. On the other hand, any breakup of the Soviet Union or Yugoslavia is likely to be accompanied by expanded trade, since the breakaway republics are likely to trade more with the West.

The big trade impact will come instead from a dramatic reorientation of trade toward the West, and toward the European Community and Germany in particular. Assuming that EESU develop in a manner similar to certain comparator countries in Europe and do not face trade barriers in the European Community, trade with these countries will amount to more than a quarter of EC trade in the long run, up from 4 percent to 5 percent currently. The corresponding number for Czechoslovakia, Hungary, and Poland alone is around 7 percent (up from less than 1 percent). The natural trade partners of EESU are the advanced industrial countries of Europe, rather than each other. The United States and Japan will be affected much less than the European Community. Our predictions, based on interwar trade patterns as well as the experience of comparator countries, imply a very sharp fall in bilateral trade between the Soviet Union and the EE6. These predictions also receive support from current developments in the trade of the region: EESU are rapidly reorienting their trade toward the West. On the whole, this will be a source of welfare gain for the West, as it will create new markets and new sources of imports.

However, we think that the predicted reorientation toward EC markets, even in the absence of large increases in EESU incomes, is too large to be accommodated comfortably. The implied market penetration levels are simply too high. Therefore, two outcomes are likely. First, EC restrictions on trade with EESU (in agriculture, textiles and clothing, and steel) will remain and possibly multiply. Second, some of the increase in EC imports from EESU will come at the expense of the exports of non-European countries.

There is a sharp difference in the comparative advantage patterns exhibited by the Soviet Union and by the Eastern European countries. In the case of the Soviet Union, we will see trade aligned neatly along intersectoral lines: the country will export natural resources and energy and import manufactures and food. The comparative advantage pattern of the Eastern European countries looks more like that of the middle-income developing countries. They have strong export potential in certain consumer goods and light manufactures, as well as in agricultural items in the cases of Poland, Hungary, and Romania. A large expansion of exports intensive in human capital is unlikely unless capital inflows to the region increase appreciably.

Hence, as far as trade flows are concerned, the external impact will be mainly an EC matter. The EC countries will face both challenges and opportunities. The integration of EESU into the world economy will create new markets for exports but will also likely raise tensions in sensitive sectors such as agriculture and some manufactures.

As EESU become integrated into the world economy, they will tend to compete most directly with the middle-income countries; these include some of the Mediterranean countries, the East Asian newly industrializing countries, and the more industrialized Latin American countries. These countries, and particularly the last two groups, are likely to see their exports partially displaced from EC markets. Moreover, unlike the advanced countries, these countries will not be able to make up for lost markets by increasing their exports to EESU themselves.

3 Consequences for Capital Flows and Macroeconomic Performance

How will developments in Eastern Europe and the Soviet Union affect world capital markets? Should we expect a massive flow of funds from the developed economies to these economies in transition? Some studies have discussed amounts in excess of $400 billion per year to the countries in Eastern Europe over the coming decade—possibly more once the Soviet Union is included! Will these flows push up world interest rates, crowding out investment in the industrialized countries and contributing to a slowdown in world growth? Will they come at the expense of the developing countries, as a limited supply of resources simply gets shifted from one group of recipients to another? These are among the concerns of those who fear that transition in the East will prove costly to the West—and particularly to the South.

At the other end of the spectrum are those who argue that developments in the East will have little or no effect on world capital markets—especially in the short to medium run. In most of EESU there is extreme uncertainty about when—and whether—key steps will be undertaken. In this view, this uncertainty means that private capital is unlikely to flock to the region. Flows may be forthcoming from the international financial institutions and Western governments, but the amounts—with the exception of German support for the development of the former East Germany—are likely to be modest at best.

To some extent, these two views focus on different aspects of the same question. Most of those expressing concern do so from the perspective of the developing countries, whereas most of those arguing that the impact will be small base their analysis on implications for the United States or the developed countries as a whole. Those concerned about the short-run implications are less likely to be awed by the numbers than those who focus on the very long run. Analyses have also differed in their implicit assumptions about the determinants of international capital flows. Some assume that the capital flows needed to finance additional investment in EESU will be forthcoming. Others assume that limitations on these capital flows will constrain the amount of investment that these economies will be able to undertake.

There may be some truth in both sets of conclusions. It will be important to take a disaggregated look at the world economy in order to assess them adequately. More generally, we will need to distinguish among a number of different groups in our analysis. We have already pointed out the great differences between the Soviet Union and Eastern Europe, and among the economies in Eastern Europe. In addition, the potential sources of funds to the region—including the private sector, the international institutions, and governments—differ greatly in their likely response. It is especially difficult to assess the private-sector response. To this end, we have conducted a survey of large firms, the results of which, presented in more detail in appendix C, provide some information about the likely investment activities of private Western firms in the region.

The section that follows sets out a simple framework that relates transformation in the East to interest rates and investment in the West and in particular to the resources available for developing countries. Applying the framework requires both estimates of the likely capital flows to EESU and estimates of the determinants of world interest rates. These estimates are developed in the second and third sections of the chapter: first we discuss estimates of the net resource transfer to EESU under both a full catch-up scenario and a more realistic scenario; we then estimate interest elasticities of saving and investment in the developed countries, to help us pin down the trade-off between interest rates and total transfers; we also estimate the relationship between investment in the developing countries and the net resource transfer they receive. The penultimate section brings these estimates together to quantitatively assess the macroeconomic implications of transition. We emphasize that these numerical estimates are meant to be suggestive only and are subject to a number of uncertainties. In the same section we also discuss the implications for particular groups of countries. Concluding remarks are provided in the chapter's final section.

A Framework for Analysis

This section sets out a simple framework for analyzing the macroeconomic implications of EESU transition. By design, it is overly simplistic and requires a number of strong assumptions. However, its main purpose is to establish a basis for discussion. Its key parameters are estimated below.

The framework illustrates a central point, namely, that any new net resource transfer from the industrial countries as a group to EESU must come from one of two sources: reduced transfers from the industrial to the developing countries, or increased net saving within the industrial countries. The latter would be generated by a rise in real interest rates, reducing domestic investment and (possibly) increasing saving.

We divide the world into three regions: the developed countries (D), the developing countries or LDCs (L), and EESU. Capital markets in D and L are not fully integrated. However, both the public and the private sector in D transfer resources to L. Throughout our discussion, we focus on *net* resource transfers—the current account balance net of debt-service payments. This is the appropriate measure of the external resources available for financing domestic investment, which is one of our central concerns. (Net transfers from D to L may be negative, as in the actual post–1982 experience.)

Initially, EESU are isolated from the other two regions, both in terms of international trade and in terms of international capital movements. Then EESU transformation occurs, introducing new, attractive investment opportunities for Western capital owners. During the transition, EESU become additional (potential) recipients for developed-country capital flows, competing with L for those flows. Investment in EESU may also push up interest rates in D, crowding out investments that would otherwise have taken place there.

In the long run, our full catch-up scenario assumes that the transition is successful, so that EESU effectively become like D and both goods and capital markets are fully integrated between D and EESU. An alternative approach would have been to assume fully integrated capital markets (between D and EESU) *during* the transition. This would imply equalization of expected real returns across the regions and, as discussed further in the next section, potentially massive capital flows from D into EESU. We find this scenario extremely implausible—especially for the next few years—and not a useful benchmark for discussing the likely short- to medium-run implications for regional saving, investment, interest rates, and international capital movements.

Figure 3.1 illustrates the situation prior to EESU transformation. The first and second panels show aggregate saving (S) and investment (I), both as shares of GDP, in D and in L, respectively, as functions of real interest rates (r). (Other determinants of saving and investment are discussed below.) In the absence of net resource transfers between regions, real interest rates will be higher in L than in D, reflecting a larger number of high-return investments relative to regional saving in L than in D. We assume that L is credit constrained, in the sense that capital flows between L and D do not equalize interest rates across regions.

Suppose that there is a net resource transfer of T_1 (measured in terms of developed-country GDP) from D to L. The corresponding interest rate in D is then r_1. Investment in L is I_1^L, as developing-country savings are augmented by the transfer (in terms of developing-country GDP), to finance investment. The (shadow) return to capital in L is r_1^L. This is shown in the first two panels of figure 3.1. The third panel, which depicts the set of possible combinations of net resource transfers and interest rates, shows that larger net transfers to the developing countries are associated with higher real interest rates in the developed-country capital market,[1] as well as greater investment and a lower cost of capital in the developing countries. Thus, the framework identifies a trade-off between interest rates and net capital flows to developing countries. (Of course, factors that shift developed-country saving and investment schedules will also shift this trade-off.) The framework does not specify where along that trade-off the world economy will end up, except in the limiting case with perfect capital mobility and no debt repudiation

---

1. Note that some policy changes that result in a higher net resource transfer may shift the developed-country saving or investment schedule. For example, if an official debt reduction were associated with increased public saving in developed countries, it need not result in higher interest rates.

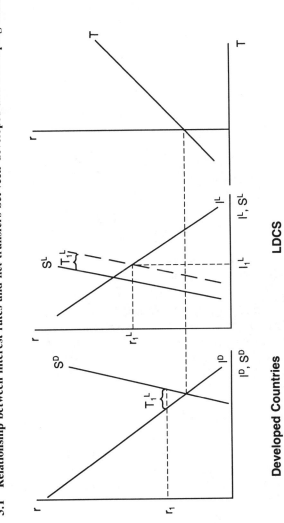

FIGURE 3.1 Relationship between interest rates and net transfers between developed and developing countries

FIGURE 3.2   Effect of transformation in Eastern Europe and the Soviet Union on interest rates and net transfers to developing countries

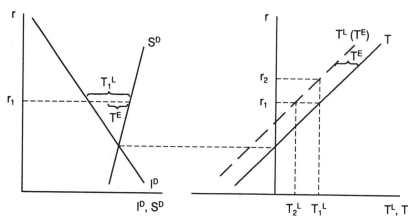

problems or absorptive constraints in the developing countries (i.e., with interest rates equalized).

What happens when economic transition in EESU introduces new potential recipients for capital from D? The outcome depends on two factors: first, the magnitude of the resulting net transfers to EESU, and second, the magnitude of the changes, if any, in total resource transfers from D to EESU and L combined. Let us suppose that T^E is the net transfer from D to EESU. As in L, investment in EESU is determined by internal saving plus the transfer, and internal real interest rates will exceed real interest rates in the international capital market.

The new situation is illustrated in figure 3.2. The left panel again shows saving and investment in D and interest rates in international capital markets. The right panel shows the relationship between interest rates and the total transfer from D as before. It also shows (dashed line) the relationship between interest rates and the net transfer from D to L, given T^E.

The key point in figure 3.2 is that the locus of possible combinations of interest rates and net resource transfers to the developing economies shifts, and the size of the shift is directly related to the net capital flows to the East. Each level of net transfer to L is now associated with a higher real interest rate in the developed-country capital markets than before the EESU transition. Higher interest rates generate resources for the transfer in part through reduced developed-country investment. At one extreme, if interest rates are to be kept at r_1, the net transfer to the developing countries must fall to T_2^L. At the other extreme, if the level of transfer to L is left unchanged at T_1^L, interest rates in the developed countries must rise from r_1 to r_2 as the amount of the combined transfer increases.

How much real interest rates must rise to maintain a given level of transfer to L depends on the sensitivity of saving and investment in the developed region to interest rates and on the magnitude of capital flows to the East. For example, if both saving and investment are relatively insensitive to interest rates, any increase in transfers to EESU will mean that interest rates must rise substantially to maintain the initial net resource transfer to L. Alternatively, capital flows to L would have to be cut substantially for interest rates to remain at their initial levels.

Our framework highlights the point that any new net resource transfer from D to EESU must come either from increased net saving in D (associated with a rise in interest rates) or from reduced transfers to L, or from a combination of the two. The rest of this chapter operationalizes this framework: first we assess the likely size of the net resource transfer to EESU; we then estimate the interest elasticities of saving and investment in D as well as the sensitivity of investment in L to the transfer from D; finally we combine these analyses to arrive at quantitative implications of EESU transition for interest rates, interregional transfers, and investment in L. We also discuss, in qualitative terms, the differing welfare implications for different regions of the world economy.

Estimates of Capital Flows to Eastern Europe and the Soviet Union

To operationalize the above framework, we must first estimate how large net capital flows from the West to the East will be. Any response must be highly speculative, especially over the medium to long run. There have been at least three approaches to estimating the likely size of these flows: "needs-based" calculations, Marshall Plan–based schemes, and sources-of-capital estimates. Needs-based calculations provide the full catch-up scenario for capital flows. As discussed below, we believe that this approach suggests inconceivably large transfers to the region. We discuss it primarily to show where the estimates of massive capital flows advanced by some analysts have their origin. In addition, there have been many calls for an assistance plan for EESU modeled on the Marshall Plan for Western Europe after World War II. Thus, it is interesting to look back at the magnitudes of assistance provided by the original plan and to ask what they might imply today.

However, neither of these approaches specifies precisely where these capital flows might come from. In our view, this is a critical issue over the next few years. Thus, we also look at the various potential sources of funds individually, and we make educated guesses about the magnitudes of capital forthcoming from each. This last set of figures is the most useful for assessing the short-term implications of EESU transition.

"NEEDS-BASED" APPROACHES: A FULL CATCH-UP SCENARIO

Some recent studies have attempted to assess the capital needs of the economies in transition, and have used these estimates to project capital inflows from the West under the (in our view unjustified) assumption that *all* of the region's investment will have to be financed externally. These studies have used one of two methods. The first uses ballpark estimates of labor productivity in EESU to estimate its current capital stock, and then estimates "needed" capital accumulation as the amount required to bring EESU's capital-labor ratios to current levels in the West. The second assumes a target real income growth rate for the region and a capital-output ratio to be achieved after a decade of growth in order to pin down "needed" capital accumulation.[2]

---

2. For example, the study by the Centre for Economic Policy Research (1990) uses a "target growth" approach to assess capital needs, and assumes that all investment is financed by foreign capital. A Congressional Budget Office (1990) study discusses both types of needs-based approaches but rejects their implied capital inflows as unrealistic. Alexander and Gagnon (1990) employ a more complex version of the labor productivities

In the previous chapter, our full catch-up scenario made assumptions about long-run income levels in EESU and examined the implications for trade flows in the long run. The needs-based approaches also begin with assumptions about long-run income (or capital stocks). But here there are strong implications for capital flows during the transition. We view the short-run capital flow implications of these approaches as extremely implausible—even if one is optimistic about the prospects for EESU to catch up with the West.

Consider first the labor productivity approach. Suppose that capital accumulation in EESU will be enough to raise the capital-labor ratio in the region to the current average among developed countries within 10 years (the time frame chosen by the CEPR study). The required annual capital accumulation depends on the difference between the initial capital stock and the 10-year target level. If the relationship among labor, capital, and output in EESU after transition is just like the currently observed relationship in the developed economies, then this difference can be estimated given a few key parameters.

If labor is currently half as productive in EESU as it is among developed economies on average, for example, then the capital-labor ratio in the East is about one-eighth the capital-labor ratio in the developed West, given a capital coefficient of about one-third. We assume a capital-output ratio of 2.5 in the West, and use actual output data for the West and labor force data for the East and the West to solve for the implied capital stocks. In particular, we assume GDP is \$13.6 trillion in the developed countries and that labor forces (in millions of workers) are 396, 56, and 155, respectively, in the three regions.[3]

These figures imply an initial capital stock of roughly \$600 billion in Eastern Europe alone and \$2.3 trillion in EESU combined.[4] To attain

approach in calibrating the eastern German economy for their multicountry simulation model. They determine capital inflows for German unification endogenously.

3. These data come from Central Intelligence Agency (1989).

4. Assume $Y = AK^\alpha L^{(1-\alpha)}$, or $Y/L = A(K/L)^\alpha$, where $= 1/3$, $K^D/Y^D = 2.5$, and $A = 7.8$. Capital stocks in the East can then be calculated as one-eighth the capital-labor ratio in the developed countries times the labor force in the East. This implies initial capital Tstocks (in billions of dollars) of $(1/8) \times 56 \times (34,000/396) = 601$ for Eastern Europe alone, and $(1/8) \times (56 + 155) \times (34,000/396) = 2,264$ for EESU.

TABLE 3.1   **Eastern Europe and the Soviet Union: estimates of investment needs** (billions of dollars per year)[a]

Method	Eastern Europe	Soviet Union	Total
Labor productivity approach	420.7	1,164.1	1,584.8
Target growth approach	344.2	571.1	915.3

a. Estimates of annual capital inflows needed over a 10-year period to bring EESU's capital-labor ratios to Western levels (labor productivity approach) or to achieve a real income growth target of 7 percent (target growth approach). See text for explanation of methodology.

the same labor productivity as the West in 10 years would require a sevenfold increase in these capital stocks. As shown in table 3.1, this would imply net capital accumulation of approximately $420 billion per year for EE6 alone, and more than $1.5 trillion per year if the Soviet Union is included as well.

We note that these figures are based on a high estimate of the relative labor productivity in EESU.[5] Using the methodology above, lower relative labor productivity assumptions would reduce our estimate of current capital stocks in the region, and consequently increase "needs-based" estimates of investment figures. On the other hand, a longer catch-up period would reduce the required annual capital inflows.

The alternative method begins by targeting an annual average growth rate for the region. Suppose output grew in real terms by 7 percent per year, a feat that has been accomplished by some of the Asian countries. Then Eastern Europe's real GDP would rise to about $1.4 trillion by 2001. Assuming the same capital-output ratio of 2.5, this would require a capital stock of $3.44 trillion in 10 years, or about $344 billion per

---

5. The IMF (1990b) assumes that labor in eastern Germany is 35 percent as productive as labor in western Germany. Giustiniani et al. (1991) assume this figure is 25 percent. They also assume that labor in Czechoslovakia, Romania, Hungary, and Poland are 31 percent, 24 percent, 23 percent, and 19 percent, respectively, as productive as labor in Austria.

year capital accumulation for Eastern Europe (table 3.1). Including the Soviet Union, the annual accumulation increases to $915 billion. Although these figures are smaller than the ones discussed above, they are still extremely large.[6]

Clearly capital accumulations of this magnitude, if all externally financed, imply massive flows to the region. The estimate of $420 billion is more than 3 percent of annual output from the developed countries, and more than 14 percent of their current investment. The analysis in the following sections suggests that flows of this range would either cause skyrocketing interest rates, or wreak havoc on investment in the developing countries—or both.

"Needs-based" approaches present an extremely misleading impression of likely capital flows for a number of reasons. First, $420 billion is more than 60 percent of current output in Eastern Europe. It is inconceivable that the region could productively invest sums of that magnitude, especially during the early years of an extremely complex transition. Even if investment is assumed to increase over the decade, this scenario implies investment levels in excess of 40 percent of output on average.

Second, inflows of this magnitude imply unsustainably large increases in the region's external debt. Even if fully half of the flows were grants or direct investments, an inconceivably large amount, the region would have accumulated an additional debt of more that 100 percent of its GNP by 2001. For comparison, the average debt–GDP ratio for 15 countries described by the World Bank as "heavily indebted" was less than 40 percent in 1990.

Third, there is no reason to assume that all of the capital accumulation that will take place will be financed externally. In fact, the history of economic development suggests that internal saving, not capital inflows from abroad, make up the bulk of investment finance. Data for the Eastern European countries suggest that roughly 20 percent to 25 per-

---

6. CEPR (1990) follows a similar methodology but takes a smaller initial income level for Eastern Europe, and therefore calculates smaller annual capital needs, ranging from $132 billion to $291 billion per year over the course of a decade.

cent of output has been invested in recent years.[7] If the transition is to be successful, these resources will need to be channeled toward productive investments. And 25 percent of output may be a more reasonable target for annual capital accumulation.

Fourth, this framework assumes that all of the increased labor productivity must come through higher physical capital-labor ratios. However, it is widely believed that large increases in output, using existing resources, may be made possible simply by introducing flexible prices and markets that allocate those resources efficiently, together with the introduction of technologies from the West. Note that the production function in footnote 4 above and existing capital and labor resources in Eastern Europe imply an output of $1.34 trillion, nearly twice the current level. Clearly, the current production function in EESU is very different from that operating in the OECD. Perhaps the real message here concerns the importance of technical assistance for the region.

Finally, this framework assumes that all of the adjustment takes place through capital accumulation in EESU. Some of the differences in economic conditions in Eastern versus Western Europe may instead be reduced through migration of labor to the West. Indeed, this remains a major concern of governments in the European Community.

MARSHALL PLAN–BASED ESTIMATES

There have been many calls for a Marshall Plan for Eastern Europe. The argument is that the United States' transfer of capital to Western Europe after World War II provides a model for Western help to revive the economies of Eastern Europe.[8] In fact, the actual role the Marshall Plan played in reviving economic growth in postwar Western Europe is far from clear. Evidence suggests that reforms were already in progress in most recipients, and that recovery had already begun—for exam-

---

7. These figures combine Economic Commission for Europe (1990) estimates of investment as a share of net material product with the PlanEcon estimates of GNP.

8. See Economic Commission for Europe (1990) and Kostrzewa et al. (1989) for further discussion of the Marshall Plan, and additional references.

ple, industrial production levels had started to rise—by the time the aid funds actually arrived. Furthermore, there is little evidence that the countries that received the most aid sustained stronger recoveries. West Germany received relatively little Marshall Plan assistance but enjoyed one of the strongest economic rebounds, following the 1948 reforms under Chancellor Ludwig Erhard.[9]

The Marshall Plan experience does not suggest that capital inflows—in the absence of economic reform—will lead to sustainable economic growth. Moreover, Eastern Europe as a region borrowed heavily from the West during the 1970s, and much of the capital was used to import capital equipment, without sustaining economic recovery. Between 1970 and 1981, the countries in Eastern Europe accumulated $64 billion in external debt—an average annual inflow of $5.8 billion.

It is also incorrect to suggest that the Marshall Plan provides a precedent for foreign aid tied to needed capital repletion. Marshall Plan aid was not distributed for the purpose of financing investment per se, but to address current account imbalances—what was later labeled the "dollar shortage" problem. Attempts to tie aid receipts to investment appear to have been largely unsuccessful. For example, the United Kingdom used its aid to repay its external debts. (Thus, it may be more accurate to argue that the Marshall Plan provides a precedent for tying foreign aid for Eastern Europe to outstanding levels of external debt! A Marshall Plan for Eastern Europe may come in the form of an external debt reduction, like the recent agreement between Poland and the Paris Club.)

In any case, if the industrialized countries decided to give Eastern Europe (and the Soviet Union) aid flows of the same magnitude as those conceded to Western Europe in the Marshall Plan, how large would that assistance have to be? Between April 1948 and December 1951, the Marshall Plan transferred $12.4 billion to 16 Western European countries. Most of these flows were outright grants; however, some were concessionary loans. We consider four alternatives for scaling this

---

9. Wallich (1955) provides a classic account of the 1948 German reforms. See Hansson (1990) for a more recent discussion, applied to the transition in Eastern Europe, and for additional references.

TABLE 3.2   Marshall Plan–based estimates of aid for Eastern Europe and
the Soviet Union: four alternatives (billions of dollars per
year)[a]

Method	Eastern Europe	Soviet Union	Total
Inflation adjustment	n.a.	n.a.	16.4
Real per capita adjustment	4.8	11.9	16.7
2 percent of recipient GNP	14.0	34.0	48.0
1 percent of donor GNP	n.a.	n.a.	136.0

a. It is assumed that the total amount of aid would be spread over four years, as in the
original Marshall Plan. See text for explanation of methodology.

$12.4 billion up to the current situation. The results are shown in table
3.2. First, we simply adjust for inflation using the US GNP deflator:
$12.4 billion in 1950 is equivalent to $65.4 billion in 1989, or about
$16.4 billion per year for four years. Second, following the Economic
Commission for Europe (1990), we look at the aid needed to keep the
per capita transfer the same, again adjusted for inflation. This would
imply $4.8 billion per year ($19.2 billion total for four years) for the
EE6, or $16.7 billion per year ($66.8 billion total) for EESU.

The other two methods use GNP in the recipient or the donor countries as the basis for scaling up the transfer. The Marshall Plan transfer
amounted to about 2 percent of the recipient countries' combined GNP
per year over the four years (although there was considerable variation
across countries and years). If PlanEcon's estimates of 1988 GNP are
used for the conversion, this would be about $14 billion per year ($56
billion total) for the EE6, or $48 billion per year ($192 billion total) if
the Soviet Union is included. Finally, the Marshall Plan transfer
amounted to about 1 percent of US GNP per year on average over the
four years (it reached a peak of 2.4 percent of GNP in 1949). One
percent of the current combined GNPs of the industrialized countries—
specifically, of the members of the Organization for Economic Cooperation and Development (OECD)—would be about $136 billion. Thus,
the Marshall Plan analogy could be used to generate anywhere from
quite modest to quite large assistance programs.

SOURCES OF CAPITAL

It is also possible to estimate how much capital is in fact likely to be forthcoming from potential creditors. These estimates may then be used to construct a range for the likely annual net resource transfer to EESU over the next few years of the transition. In formulating these estimates, it is important to recognize that different types of creditors may respond quite differently to developments in EESU. First there are the international financial institutions, whose mandate involves lending to member countries. Hungary, Poland, Romania, Yugoslavia, and (since 1990) Bulgaria and Czechoslovakia are IMF and World Bank members. Governments in the developed countries also lend to the region for a combination of political and economic reasons. These official assistance efforts are being coordinated through the G-24, composed of the 24 members of the OECD and the Commission of the European Communities. In addition there are private creditors, including commercial banks and private firms. Their investments are presumably determined by risk assessments and expected returns.

There are also important differences among the potential borrowers. In particular, the Soviet Union does not belong to the international financial institutions and is an especially uncertain environment for private investors. Eastern Germany, on the other hand, appears certain to receive very large capital inflows. However, it is in a special position vis-à-vis the former West Germany, and much of its transition will be financed by transfers within the unified Germany. Thus, we look at these two economies separately from the rest of the region in order to formulate a sensible estimate of the magnitude of capital flows.

The EE6

Table 3.3 provides estimates of gross official and multilateral capital flows for the remaining six countries of Eastern Europe. The first columns show projected funds from the IMF. These include financing associated with Stand-by Arrangements (SBA) or Extended Fund Facility (EFF), as well as those under the Compensatory and Contingency Financing Facility (CCFF) that is to provide emergency assistance to IMF members suffering from the 1990 oil price shock. These totals may

TABLE   3.3   Eastern Europe: prospective official and multilateral[a]
                       financing, 1991 (millions of dollars)

| | | IMF | | | | |
Country	Total	SBA and EFF	CCFF	World Bank	G-24[b]	Total
Bulgaria	713	389	324	20	1,500	2,213
Czechoslovakia	1,462	765	697	400	1,000	2,862
Hungary	1,032	726	306	400	700	2,132
Poland	734	734	0	1,100	4,000	5,834
Romania	1,238	648	590	0	700	1,938
Yugoslavia	794	794	0	0	0	794
Total	5,973	4,056	1,917	1,920	7,900	15,793

CCFF = Compensatory and Contingency Financing Facility; EFF = Extended Fund Facility; SBA = Stand-By Agreement.

a. Drawings from the IMF and the World Bank could be delayed past 1991.

b. Includes balance of payments assistance that has been discussed for Czechoslovakia and Hungary. Figures for Bulgaria and Romania are conjectural. Figures for Poland and Bulgaria reflect the likely value of Paris Club rescheduling as of February 1991.

Source: US Department of State, February 1991.

overstate the actual amount of drawings from the IMF during 1991. In particular, Romania hopes to sign an SBA but has not done so as of this writing. New programs for Poland and Hungary will also need to be finalized.[10] The table also shows prospective lending from the World Bank in 1991. The total projection for assistance from these sources is

10. One-year SBAs were approved for Hungary and Poland in February and March 1990, respectively. New agreements are being negotiated. Yugoslavia embarked on an 18-month SBA in March 1990. SBAs were approved for Czechoslovakia and Bulgaria in early 1991. Romania has negotiated a program, but it has not been formally approved as of March 1991.

$15.8 billion, about equally divided between the international financial institutions and the G-24. Note that this amount is within the range of the Marshall Plan–based flows discussed above.

Potential gross private capital flows to these countries are more difficult to estimate. Consider first foreign direct investment (FDI). Plan-Econ estimates suggest that Hungary received slightly more than $300 million in 1990, whereas Poland received $400 million in the first quarter of 1990 alone (*PlanEcon Report*, various issues). If these flows continued, the two countries would have attracted more than $1.5 billion in FDI over the year. Extrapolating from this figure, we would view $3 billion as a high estimate of total FDI to the region during 1990, and $2 billion to $5 billion as a reasonable, if perhaps optimistic, range for annual FDI in the early to mid-1990s. Of course, if the investment climate improves, FDI could be substantially higher.

Although it is difficult to infer aggregate flows from a small sample of firms, the $2 billion to $5 billion range also appears to be consistent with the responses from our private-sector survey (see appendix C). Since the respondents were primarily large international firms, which would be the most likely to consider investing in Eastern Europe, we used their responses to construct an upper bound. Our calculations suggest that the responding firms anticipate at most a 65 percent increase in their annual investments in Eastern Europe (excluding the former East Germany) over the next five years. A 65 percent rise from a $3 billion total inflow would be slightly less than $5 billion. Since both the 65 percent and the $3 billion were calculated to be on the high side, we take $5 billion per year as our upper bound on FDI flows to Eastern Europe for the near term.

Table 3.4 provides some information about past medium- and long-term private-sector financing to the region. It shows that publicized bank credits and bond issues have varied considerably from year to year, averaging $2.2 billion per year during 1985–89. Hungary has received the lion's share of the flows to Eastern Europe, with Bulgaria a distant second, followed by Czechoslovakia.

However, Eastern Europe's borrowing on international financial markets fell sharply in 1990. Credit standings have been downgraded, and unless economic performance improves substantially there is little reason to expect large increases in flows in the short term. Total use of

TABLE 3.4   Eastern Europe and the Soviet Union: international medium-
and long-term financing obtained through publicized bank
credits or bond issues, 1985–90 (millions of dollars)

Country	1985	1986	1987	1988	1989	1990
Bulgaria	475	45	260	194	580	–
Czechoslovakia	100	278	242	330	334	377
Hungary	1,642	1,315	1,951	1,016	1,334	990
Poland	–	–	30	–	163	–
Romania	150	–	–	–	–	–
Total	2,367	1,638	2,483	1,540	2,785	1,367
Soviet Union[a]	1,508	1,821	1,003	2,679	1,858	290
CMEA banks	250	400	20	75	75	–
Total	4,125	3,859	3,506	4,294	4,718	3,024
Memoranda: terms of syndicated credits						
Average margin (basis points over LIBOR)	55	26	24	30	49	–
Average maturity (months)	89	89	97	101	99	–

LIBOR = London interbank offer rate.

a. Excludes a DM5 billion loan extended in 1990 by German banks and carrying the guarantee of the Federal Republic of Germany.

Source: OECD (1991, table 12, p. 30).

bonds and syndicated loans fell from $2.8 billion in 1989 to just $1.4 billion in 1990. The following assessment appears to be valid:

Hungary and Czechoslovakia still maintain some access to the public markets, but other countries will have to rely on bank-to-bank private credits, trade finance or officially supported credits. The participants in the private markets would clearly wish to become involved in the development of market economies in the region, but through activities such as investment banking, project finance and dealing with the emerging private sector, rather than through the traditional sovereign credits and bonds.

However, strong private borrowers and a sufficient number of good projects have yet to emerge. (OECD 1990, 8)

We will consider a range of $1 billion to $5 billion per year for potential commercial credit to the region over the next few years. Again, this may be on the optimistic side. It allows for a substantial rise in private-sector credit if the transition proceeds well. The downside risk is that banks will continue their attempts to reduce exposure to the region.

These figures suggest that the EE6 could expect to receive $18 billion to $26 billion in gross flows in 1991. To estimate the likely net transfer, we also need to consider debt-service payments from the region. If all existing debt (before Poland's debt reduction) were serviced, payments would be about $7.5 billion for 1991. However, likely service payments will be considerably lower. Poland and Bulgaria have not been servicing their debts, and many observers wonder whether Yugoslavia will continue to pay in full. In any case, if only Czechoslovakia, Hungary, Romania, and Yugoslavia make payments, the total would be about $3.5 billion. Poland has just reached an agreement with the Paris Club to reduce its official debt (currently about $35 billion) by at least 50 percent, and the final reduction may reach 70 percent. When this agreement is complete, Poland is likely to resume servicing its remaining official debt. Thus, we take the potential range of total debt service from these countries to be from $3 billion to $7 billion.

These figures imply that $12 billion to $24 billion is a reasonable range for annual net resource transfers to the countries of Eastern Europe over the early to mid-1990s.[11] This range could be viewed as similar to the Marshall Plan transfers to Western Europe. Note that a $12 billion net inflow could come even if there is no additional private capital (e.g., $15.8 official inflows net of a $3.5 billion debt service). Our range is somewhat higher than the estimate by Diwan (1990) in a similar exercise. He predicts gross flows of $14.6 billion per year—with just $7.8 billion and $0.7 billion from public sources and FDI, respectively, but surpris-

---

11. Are net inflows reasonable in light of Poland's recent trade surpluses? We would argue that they are. We expect that Poland will need to go from its present surpluses to (small) deficits to undertake needed investments and to revive economic growth.

ingly large commercial flows to the region, including $1.3 billion each to Bulgaria and Czechoslovakia and $2 billion to Poland—and net flows of roughly $8 billion. However, the range we arrive at is similar to the $10 billion to $20 billion range that the CBO (1990) considers reasonable.

Some would argue that flows of this magnitude are too large in the sense that these countries may prove unable to service the implied accumulation in their external debts. However, the reasons for this concern are not at all obvious. If the countries are able to raise their incomes—and especially their exports—servicing an additional $16 billion in loans per year should be quite manageable. Recall that our medium-term scenario from chapter 2 suggested that merchandise exports could grow from $90 billion in 1989 to $135 billion over the next three to five years.

A different concern is that these inflows are too small to achieve the desired economic transition. It is certainly true that flows of this magnitude will not enable these countries to achieve capital-labor ratios like those in the European Community over the next decade, and that the lion's share of domestic investments will need to be financed by domestic saving. However, this does not preclude more modest, but still impressive, success in raising domestic living standards.

Soviet Union

It is even more difficult to get a handle on likely flows to the Soviet Union. The country has been able to attract substantial capital inflows in the past. Table 3.4 shows medium- and long-term financing of $2.7 billion in 1988 and $1.7 billion in 1989. However, the Soviet Union's external situation has deteriorated. Many Soviet importers have accumulated substantial arrears on repayment of trade credits. As the country's credit rating has declined, interest rate spreads charged by financial institutions have risen (to over 1 percentage point in January 1991). The Soviet Union borrowed little from international capital markets during 1990 (Commission of the European Communities 1990). Recent IMF estimates suggest that net capital flows (in convertible currencies) to the Soviet Union were about $1 billion in 1988 and $3.5 billion in 1989. These flows appear to have dropped sharply to $ − 9.8 billion in the first half of 1990—a net capital outflow. This reversal was due almost exclusively to large short-term capital outflows (Commission of the European Communities 1990, table A.1). However, if reforms proceed, the large Soviet market could make it an attractive place for private investors, and the level of official capital flows could increase. As of this writing, however, only Germany has committed assistance.

We will consider a range of $ − 4 billion to $6 billion for net flows to the Soviet Union. In the pessimistic scenario, net outflows continue. In the optimistic scenario, private inflows rise substantially.

German Unification

The financing of German unification is quite a different story from either that of the EE6 or that of the Soviet Union. We call it unification, and not flows to eastern Germany, to highlight the point that much of the transfer is expected to come from increased net saving in western Germany and to result in (temporarily) higher real interest rates in Germany than elsewhere in the West.

There is an active debate over whether Germany should finance some or all of the reconstruction in its eastern part through higher taxes and reductions in expenditure on other items.[12] Thus, we focus on the net financing requirement of the German government, under the assumption that it will contribute very large amounts for development of eastern Germany. Given the overall strength of the western German economy, and the Federal Republic's and the Bundesbank's excellent reputation for maintaining economic stability, we assume that the German government will be able to finance its expenditures in the eastern part of the country. In this sense, the "needs-based" approach considered above is more applicable for Germany than for the EE6 or the Soviet Union.

A wide range of estimates have been calculated for the German government's net borrowing requirement related to unification. For example, CBO (1990) puts the net borrowing costs at 5 percent of united Germany's GDP (about $50 billion) or less, depending on how much is

---

12. Some tax increases were approved in Germany shortly before this study went to press. However, substantial uncertainties about future tax revenues and about the costs of restructuring the eastern part of the country remain.

TABLE   3.5   **Eastern Europe and the Soviet Union: net capital flows under three alternative scenarios** (billions of dollars per year)[a]

Recipient	Scenario		
	I	II	III
Eastern Europe	12	18	24
Soviet Union	−4	2	6
German unification	22	35	60
Total	30	55	90

a. Scenario I takes the lower bounds for author's estimates of likely net capital flows to each recipient. Scenario III takes the upper bounds. Scenario II provides an intermediate case. See text for methodology.

financed by tax increases. The IMF (1990b) estimates that eastern Germany will require $44 billion from global saving to finance external imbalances in 1991 (falling to $34 billion by 1995), but assumes that a full two-thirds will come from western Germany, leaving just $15 billion to come from the rest of the industrialized countries in 1991. This figure is well below most other estimates and appears low for our purposes, since we want to account for some of the spillover effects of higher interest rates within Germany.[13] We take a wide range—$22 billion to $60 billion per year—to emphasize the uncertainties here. As these figures suggest, German unification could swamp the effects of developments in the other countries.

THREE SCENARIOS

Table 3.5 combines our estimates of the likely net flows from various sources so as to construct three scenarios. The first scenario takes the lower bounds of all of our ranges. This implies an annual net capital

---

13. The Alexander and Gagnon (1990) simulations suggest that $125 billion in additional annual investment over the next decade will be associated with German unification, but that this will result in a deterioration of at most $29 billion per year in Germany's current account balance.

flow of $30 billion to EESU. The second scenario shows an intermediate case that appears to us to be a reasonable guess of the likely outcome, with a net annual capital flow to the region of $55 billion, reflecting moderate flows to Germany. The third scenario combines large flows to EESU together with large borrowings to finance German unification to imply an upper bound of $90 billion per year. Note that even the largest of these numbers is still a fraction of the magnitudes estimated from the "needs-based" approach. They are, however, in the ballpark of a "Marshall Plan," providing from 1.5 percent to 4.3 percent of total recipient GNP. However, the sums are distributed very unequally, with Germany receiving most of the inflows, and the Soviet Union receiving far less than the rest of Eastern Europe.

Investment, Saving, and Interest Rates: Econometric Evidence

Our next step is to examine the determinants of investment and saving in the developed and the developing countries. In particular, we wish to find out how changes in interest rates in international capital markets are related to developed-country saving and investment. This will enable us to quantify the interest rate consequences of the capital flows discussed above. We also wish to find out how sensitive developing-country investment is to the net resource transfer from the developed countries. We then turn to a discussion of the actual changes in interest rates that have occurred since the transition in EESU began.

ESTIMATION RESULTS

Using annual data from 1960 to 1988, we estimated determinants of saving and investment, both as shares of GDP, for the developed countries as a group and for the developing countries as a group.[14] We

---

14. All data used in the regressions below come from the IMF, *International Financial Statistics,* various issues, except those for the net resource transfer to developing countries, which come from the World Bank. We use the IMF definition of developing countries, and their industrial countries as our developed countries.

describe investment levels in the developed countries (I^D) as dependent on four factors: a measure of real interest rates (r), real economic growth (*GRWTH*), and indices of wages (*WAGE*) and oil prices (*POIL*), both adjusted for the overall price level in the region. We tried using current and lagged interest rates, and both short- and long-term interest rates. The best fit was for real long-term rates with a one-year lag (r_{-1}).[15] These estimation results, which are corrected for serial correlation, are reported below (with *t*-statistics in parentheses).

(3.1)

$$I^D = 0.205 - 0.226\, r_{-1} + 0.448\; GRWTH - 0.142\; WAGE + 0.004\; POIL$$
$$(8^\prime.63)\;\; (-4.51) \qquad (7.66) \qquad\quad (-7.05) \qquad\quad (1.81)$$

$$\text{adjusted } R^2 = 0.97$$

The estimates in equation (3.1) show that investment among the developed countries declines as real interest rates rise. However, investment is not very sensitive to interest rates. A 1-percentage-point rise in real interest rates (say, from 4 percent to 5 percent) would decrease investment by less than a quarter of a percent of GDP—for example, from 18.23 percent to 18.00 percent. This low elasticity simply reflects the fact that although world real interest rates have fluctuated considerably over the past two decades, there have been only small changes in industrial-country investment behavior. In terms of figure 3.1, it appears that the developed-country investment schedule is quite steep.[16] The estimates also show that investment increases with higher rates of real growth. Declines in real wages increase investment, pre-

---

15. Our measure of long-term real interest rates is a GNP–weighted average of yields on US, German, and Japanese government bonds, less the percentage change in the industrial-country GDP deflator. we also tried the London interbank offer rate (LIBOR), adjusted for inflation, as a measure of short-term real interest rates. Because of the potential for endogeneity, we used instrumental variable techniques when including current interest rates, or correcting for serial correlation.

16. The estimated interest elasticity of investment is even smaller (0.14) when we use a short-term real rate in our regressions. Note, however, that low-interest elasticities for the developed countries as a group does not necessarily translate into low elasticities for each individual country.

sumably because profits rise. On balance, higher oil prices are associated with slight increases in investment. This finding may reflect increased liquidity in international financial markets when oil prices rose in the 1970s.

Taking aggregate saving as the difference between income and (public plus private) consumption, we infer determinants of developed-country saving from the consumption side. Our equation for consumption (C^D, again measured as a share of GDP) includes four explanatory variables. The first is real interest rates (r) as above. Again, we tried both current and lagged, and both short- and long-term rates, and we used instrumental variable techniques where appropriate. We report below the results using current long-term real interest rates. For the second variable, we allowed changes in fiscal policy to influence aggregate consumption by including the average budget deficit in developed countries as a percentage of GDP (*GDEF*). Finally, we separated real income into a permanent (*PERM*) and a transitory (*TRANS*) component, and included both.[17] According to modern theories of consumption behavior, changes in income that are perceived to be permanent should affect consumption more (and saving less) than changes that are perceived to be transitory. The results of our consumption equation are reported below:

(3.2)

$$C^D = 0.41 + 0.037\ r + 0.760\ GDEF + 0.075\ PERM - 0.076\ TRANS$$
$$(5.8)\quad (0.33)\quad\ \ (4.97)\qquad\quad (4.81)\qquad\quad (-0.78)$$

adjusted R^2 = 0.91   Durbin-Watson = 1.7

Overall, equation (3.2) also provides a good fit. However, it finds no significant relationship between consumption and interest rates for the developed economies as a whole. We found similarly small and statistically insignificant relationships for all of the interest rate variables that we tried. This finding is consistent with the empirical literature on saving. For our purposes, the implication is that developed-country

---

17. To obtain this decomposition, we regressed current income growth on a constant and income growth lagged one and two years. The fitted values from this regression were used as "permanent" income growth, and the residuals were used as "transitory" growth.

saving is unresponsive to changes in interest rates—the saving schedule in figure 3.1 is vertical. We also find that an increase in the government budget deficit by 1 percent of GDP raises total consumption by 0.76 percent of GDP. Finally, a 1 percent boost to real growth that is perceived to be permanent tends to increase the share of income consumed slightly (by 0.075 percent). Although the relationship is not statistically significant, our estimates suggest a tendency for transitory income changes to be saved.

As discussed above, the presence of capital constraints implies that the interest rate in the developing countries will not equal that in the developed economies, and indeed, is less readily observable. However, actual investment will be determined by available financing from domestic saving plus the net resource transfer. Thus, we estimate a single reduced-form equation for the developing-country region—a standard approach in empirical work on developing countries.[18] The dependent variable is investment as a percentage of developing-country GDP (I^L). A key explanatory variable is the net resource transfer (NRT), also expressed as a percentage of developing-country GDP. We treat this variable as exogenous. We also included real income growth in the region ($GRWTHL$) and the real price of oil ($POIL$) and corrected for serial correlation.[19]

(3.3) $I^L = 0.227 + 0.780\ NRT + 0.197\ GRWTHL + 0.016\ POIL$
         (42.77)   (5.78)   (1.99)   (5.49)

    adjusted $R^2 = 0.93$

Our estimates in equation (3.3) show a strong and significant positive relationship between net resource transfers from the developed to the

---

18. For example, Cohen (1990) follows this approach. Note that the industrial-country real interest rate is positively related to investment in developing countries, which is exactly what the framework discussed in the text implies. Higher interest rates are associated with lower developed-country investment and a greater transfer to developing countries (prior to EESU transformation at least), relaxing the financing constraint on investment in the latter group.

19. We also tried a terms-of-trade index as an explanatory variable but found it to have no explanatory power.

FIGURE   3.3   **Resource transfer and investment in developing countries, 1970–87**

% GDP   % GDP

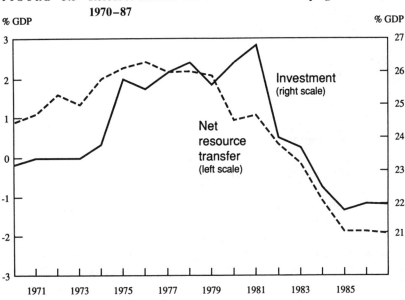

developing countries and developing-country investment expenditures. This strong relationship is also evident in figure 3.3.

What are the implications of these estimation results? First, the low interest elasticities of saving and investment in the developed countries imply a very steep trade-off between interest rates and total net resource transfers in the second panel of figure 3.2. Equation (3.4) shows the relationship between changes in interest rates and changes in the total transfer of resources to developing countries and EESU implied by our estimates.[20] Equation (3.5) shows the implied relationship between developing-country investment and the net resource transfer they receive (as a share of their income):

(3.4) $0.23\ r = (T^L + T^E) - S_0^D + I_0^D$

(3.5) $I^L = I_0^L + 0.78\ (Y^D/Y^L)\ T^L$

---

20. This follows from our empirical estimates and the fact that $S^D - I^D = T$.

In equation (3.4) S_0^D and I_0^D are components in developed-country saving and investment that are not related to interest rates, and in equation (3.5) I_0^L is the component of developing-country investment that is not related to changes in the net resource transfer.

For example, consider an increase in the total transfer to EESU plus L of \$13.2 billion, or about 0.1 percent of developed-country GDP, that is not offset by an exogenous increase in developed-country saving (a rise in S_0^D) or an exogenous decline in developed-country investment (a fall in I_0^D). Equation (3.4) implies that this would push interest rates in developed-country capital markets up by about 43 basis points (0.1/0.23). Suppose L received the entire increase in the transfer. Then, since developed-country GDP is about 4.5 times the aggregate GDP of the developing countries, equation (3.5) implies that the increased transfer to the latter would lead to a rise in investment in that region of about 0.35 percent of GDP (0.78 × 4.5 × 0.1). These relationships imply that increased transfers as a result of EESU transition could have large effects on real interest rates, or on the net transfer to developing countries. Note that the remaining discussion will be quite sensitive to these interest elasticity estimates. In particular, larger elasticities would mean that any change in transfers would be associated with smaller changes in interest rates.

RECENT CHANGES IN INTEREST RATES

Interest rates in the developed countries increased substantially following the revolutionary developments in EESU in the fall of 1989. Indeed, if market participants are forward-looking, modern theories of interest rate determination argue that they should have *already* incorporated available information about the increased investment opportunities in the transforming economies. That is, interest rates should already reflect expected future increases in world demands for capital. By 1991, higher interest rates from 1990 would reduce investment within the industrial countries, providing resources for additional transfers. Thus, the rise in interest rates from 1989 to 1990 provides us with an estimate of how markets expected developments in EESU to influence the total transfer from the developed countries.

TABLE   3.6   **World interest rates by quarter, 1989–90** (percentages per year)

| Quarter | LIBOR | Long-term rates[a] | | |
		United States	Germany	Japan
1989:II	8.32	8.77	6.97	4.99
1989:III	8.30	8.11	6.95	5.00
1989:IV	8.87	7.91	7.55	5.67
1990:I	9.14	8.42	8.57	6.97
1990:II	9.01	8.68	8.95	7.00

LIBOR = London interbank offer rate.

a. Yields on government bonds.

Source: IMF (1990a).

It is difficult to determine precisely how much real interest rates rose in response to news about EESU. Other factors influence interest rates, including macroeconomic policies within industrial countries, changing inflationary expectations, and the August 1990 Iraqi invasion of Kuwait, which led to war in early 1991. Also, different rates suggest somewhat different conclusions. We arrive at a ballpark estimate by looking at developments in LIBOR and in (nominal) long-term interest rates in the United States, Germany, and Japan between the end of 1989 and the first half of 1990. We do not look at the second half of 1990 because, by the third quarter of that year, developments in the Gulf had become a significant influence on interest rates. The relevant figures are given in table 3.6.

In the United States, long-term interest rates declined from 8.8 percent to 7.9 percent during 1989 as real economic activity slowed. They then rose by nearly 80 basis points in the first half of 1990. In Germany, interest rates were relatively stable in the second and third quarters of 1989. They jumped 60 basis points in the fourth quarter, but part of this increase is attributable to tightening Bundesbank policies. During the first half of 1990, German long-term rates rose an additional 140 basis points. Perhaps 120 to 160 basis points of the total rise from the third quarter of 1989 to mid-1990 is attributable to developments in the East, including German unification, but some may be due to related increases in inflationary expectations. Finally, Japanese long-term rates have also risen 200 basis points since mid-1989. However, at least half of this increase appears to be attributable to increased inflationary concerns or to the extreme volatility of domestic financial markets. Table 3.6 also shows that LIBOR rose 70 basis points from the third quarter of 1989 to mid-1990.[21] We will take 100 basis points as a ballpark estimate of how much real interest rates increased in response to developments in EESU during early 1990.

Macroeconomic and Regional Implications

What are the likely implications of transition in Eastern Europe and the Soviet Union for international capital markets? This section first combines the projected net capital flows to the region (table 3.5) with the estimated interest elasticities from the previous section to form a rough quantitative assessment. It then provides a more general qualitative assessment of the effects for particular regions.

QUANTITATIVE ASSESSMENT

For each of the three capital flow scenarios in table 3.5 ($30 billion, $55 billion, and $90 billion) we consider three cases representing alternative combinations of changes in interest rates and changes in the net transfer to the developing countries. These are summarized in table 3.7. The first case considers the effect on world interest rates of a transfer to EESU if the net resource transfer to the developing countries remains the same. The second considers the opposite pole of the trade-off: the effect on the net transfer to developing countries assuming real interest rates remain unchanged. Here we also show the implications for developing-country investment.

---

21. See IMF (1990b) for additional discussion of interest rate developments.

TABLE 3.7 **Implications for interest rates and net international transfers of the transition in Eastern Europe and the Soviet Union** (percentages of LDC GDP except where noted)

	Scenario[a]		
	I	II	III
Net additional transfer to EESU (billions of dollars per year)	30	55	90
Change in interest rates with unchanged net transfer to LDCs (basis points)	96	176	288
Change in net transfer to LDCs with unchanged interest rates	−1.0	−1.8	−3.0
Implied change in LDC investment	−0.8	−1.4	−2.3
Change in net transfer to LDCs given 100-basis-point rise in interest rates	0.0	−0.8	−2.0
Implied change in LDC investment	0.0	−0.6	−1.5

LDC = less developed country.

a. See table 3.5 for description of scenarios. See text for methodology.

The likely outcome will lie between these two extremes. Therefore, the third alternative, following the discussion in the previous section, assumes that real interest rates have already risen by 1 percentage point in response to developments in EESU and estimates the corresponding reduction in the net transfer to the developing countries. According to our estimates, a rise of this magnitude is consistent with an increase in *total* transfers (to developing countries and to EESU) of roughly $30 billion to $31 billion, which is 0.23 percent of industrial-country GDP (see equation 3.5). The implication is that markets expect any transfers to the East in excess of about $30 billion to be offset one-for-one with reduced transfers to the developing countries. The last rows of table 3.7 present this case.

Suppose that the additional annual net capital flows to EESU are at the low end of what we believe is plausible ($30 billion in scenario I). Our model suggests that real interest rates could rise by as much as 96 basis points if there is no accompanying reduction in flows to developing countries. Thus, the 1 percent rise in real interest rates that has actually occurred happens to be consistent with transfers of this magnitude to EESU having no adverse affect on transfers to the developing world. At the other extreme, with unchanged interest rates, the transfer to developing countries would be cut by 1.0 percent of their GDP, implying a fall in their investment of 0.8 percent of their GDP.

At the upper end of the range of possibilities that we believe is reasonable ($90 billion in scenario III), the implications of EESU transition for interest rates and for the developing countries could be much greater. Real interest rates could rise by nearly 3 percentage points if transfers to developing countries are unchanged. Alternatively, a 1-percentage-point rise in interest rates would be associated with a sharp decline in net resource transfers and investment for the developing countries—by 2.0 percent and 1.5 percent of their GDP, respectively, since their net resource transfers would fall by $60 billion. For interest rates to remain constant, transfers to and investment in the developing countries would have to fall by a striking 3.0 percent and 2.3 percent of their GDP, respectively.

Finally, consider scenario II, which we believe to be the most plausible. Here EESU receives annual transfers of $55 billion. This transfer could result in at most a 1.76-percentage-point rise in world interest rates, or at most a $55 billion cut in resources to developing countries, reducing their investment by 1.4 percent of GDP. Given the 1-percentage-point increase in interest rates that we have seen, markets appear to expect that roughly $25 billion of the $55 billion transfer to EESU will come from lower transfers to developing countries in 1991, reducing their investment by some 0.6 percent of their GDP.

Our best-guess scenario thus has four main features. First, EESU will receive net capital inflows of about $55 billion per year over the next few years. Most of this capital inflow (perhaps $40 billion) will go to finance German unification, and little if any of the remainder will go to the Soviet Union. Second, long-term real interest rates appear to have risen by about 1 percentage point in response to developments in the region. To the extent that participants in international capital markets are forward-looking, we should expect large additional interest rate movements only in response to new information. Third, our empirical estimates suggest that this rise in real interest rates is consistent with a $30 billion increase in net resource transfers from the developed countries. The implications are that $30 billion of investment has been crowded out in the developed countries (since we find saving to be insensitive to interest rates), and that the additional $25 billion in transfers to EESU will come from a reduction in transfers that would otherwise have gone to the developing countries. Fourth, this cut in resources will lower investment in the developing countries as a group by a little more than half a percent of their GDP.

These conclusions are sensitive to two factors: our estimate of the interest elasticity of investment in the developed countries and our assessment of real interest rate changes. For example, if the interest rate elasticity of investment were 0.30 instead of 0.23, the increase in net resource transfers consistent with a 100-basis-point rise in interest rates would be $41 billion instead of roughly $30 billion. In our best-guess scenario, this would imply a $14 billion reduction in transfers from the developing countries. If real interest rates rose by only 80 basis points in response to developments in the East, interest elasticities of investment of 0.23 and 0.30 would be consistent with increases in total resource transfers from the developed countries of $25 billion and $33 billion, respectively.

Finally, we note that the capital markets may not have "gotten it right." Their assessment of future transfers may not be a good prediction of how public sectors in particular will actually respond to developments in EESU. For example, if actual official transfers to EESU and the developing countries combined exceed market expectations, further increases in real interest rates could result.

REGIONAL IMPLICATIONS

So far our discussion has focused on obtaining a range of magnitudes for capital flows to EESU, and for attendant changes in interest rates and resource transfers. We have argued that the likely outcome involves higher real interest rates, increased resource transfers to EESU, and reduced transfers to developing countries. We now turn to the macro-economic implications for various groups of countries. One can identify four separate channels through which the impact will be felt: wealth effects, aggregate demand effects, growth effects, and income-distributional effects.

Wealth Effects

The increase in world interest rates has clear distributional effects across countries, the direction of which depends on the net creditor or debtor status of the country in question. Countries that are net debtors with respect to the outside world become poorer when interest rates rise, while net creditor countries become richer. The developing countries as a whole are in the first category, whereas the industrial countries as a group are in the second.

Table 3.8 shows some calculations with respect to the income losses sustained by different groups of developing countries for each 1-percentage-point increase in interest rates. These losses are proportional to the stock of outstanding debt and to the share of debt contracted at floating interest rates. To arrive at the numbers reported in the last two columns of the table, we have made the simplifying assumption that all debt contracted from private sources is at floating rates, and that none from public sources is. Moreover, the figures for debt–GDP ratios are for gross (and not net) debt, and so overstate the cost.[22] Nonetheless, the figures offer some ballpark estimates of the consequences of the increase in interest rates. In absolute terms, the biggest losers are the 15 middle-income heavily indebted countries, which in aggregate lose $3.3 billion for each 1-percentage-point rise in interest rates. Notice that, in proportion to national income, the sub-Saharan countries' losses are roughly similar to those of these middle-income countries. The reason is that the sub-Saharan countries typically have

---

22. On the other hand, increases in interest rates can also be passed on to debt contracted from official sources. This is a source of downward bias in the cost estimates.

TABLE   3.8   **Effects of an increase in world interest rates on developing countries**

	Debt as percentage of GDP (1990)	Private debt (percentages of total)	Welfare cost for each 1 percent rise in world interest rates	
			Billions of dollars	Percentages of GDP
Sub-Saharan Africa	75.7	29.8	0.36	0.23
Net debtor fuel exporters[a]	47.5	59.9	1.69	0.28
Four newly industrializing countries[b]	10.8	91.9	0.45	0.10
Fifteen heavily indebted countries[c]	37.2	66.8	3.30	0.25

a. Algeria, Cameroon, Congo, Ecuador, Gabon, Indonesia, Iraq, Mexico, Nigeria, Trinidad and Tobago, and Venezuela.

b. Hong Kong, Korea, Singapore, and Taiwan.

c. Argentina, Bolivia, Brazil, Chile, Colombia, Cote d'Ivoire, Ecuador, Mexico, Morocco, Nigeria, Peru, the Philippines, Uruguay, Venezuela, and Yugoslavia.

Source: Calculated from International Monetary Fund (1990b).

very high debt–GDP ratios, which offset their low share of borrowing from private sources.

These losses are the counterpart of income gains by the group of industrialized countries as a whole. Therefore, there is a substantial transfer of resources to the industrial world, which amounts to around $6 billion for each percentage-point increase in interest rates (this figure is obtained by adding up the losses over the four groups of developing countries in table 3.8).

However, it is also clear that not all the industrial countries gain on this account. The biggest winners are the large net creditors: Germany, Japan, and the United Kingdom. The United States, on the other hand, is in the same boat as the developing world, as it is a net external debtor.

Aggregate Demand Effects

Some observers have worried that the increase in interest rates could be recessionary, because of the effect on interest-sensitive components of aggregate demand. However, this way of looking at things starts the analysis from the wrong point. The increase in interest rates is in itself a response to an increase in spending by EESU on capital goods produced by the rest of the world. The latter shows up as an increase in the West's net exports to EESU. (Note that this is primarily a rise in Western exports to the former East Germany. The rest of EESU runs small external deficits in our short-run scenarios.) Therefore, the sign and the magnitude of the aggregate demand effect depend on the balance between the reduction in interest-sensitive spending and the increase in net exports in each country. Once again, it helps to think the issues through both at the level of industrial countries as a group, and for specific countries.

For the industrial countries as a whole, a good argument can be made that the net effect on aggregate demand will be a wash. This can be seen simply by writing the identity between net exports and net savings:

(3.6) $$S - I = X - M$$

Remember that our econometric work finds consumption, and hence saving, to be insensitive to interest rates. Therefore, S can be taken to remain unchanged in the above equation. The reduction in investment in the OECD area has to be matched by the increase in net exports (to EESU). In other words, the increase in EESU demand for capital goods has to be identical to the decline in domestic OECD demand for capital goods. For the region as a whole, the net effect on aggregate demand is nil (see appendix B for a more formal exposition on this point).

What is true for the OECD area as a whole need not be true for individual countries. Here again, we are likely to see an asymmetry between the effects on the United States and on the other OECD countries. Since the capital market is integrated within the OECD group, all of the member countries will face the same interest rate shock to domestic investment demand. However, EESU demand for imports will not be distributed uniformly across all members. As we discussed in chapter 2, the predominant share of EESU imports will come from Europe. Therefore, we would expect the incipient increase in net exports from the United States to fall short of the reduction in investment demand, and that from Europe to exceed the cut in investment demand.

Of course, the above identity has to continue to hold in every country. Two sorts of endogenous adjustments are possible to restore balance: a depreciation of the dollar relative to the European currencies; and a reduction in the level of US economic activity relative to that in Europe. Each serves to increase net import demand in Europe while decreasing it in the United States. Each makes the United States poorer and Europe richer. In practice, we are likely to see a combination of the two adjustments. (For further discussion of this issue see appendix B.)

The upshot of the trade asymmetry, therefore, is a depreciation of the dollar, a recessionary impulse in the United States, and an expansionary impulse in Europe. Note that a similar asymmetry exists within Europe also, as countries other than Germany are in a position vis-à-vis Germany similar to that of the United States vis-à-vis Europe as a whole. Therefore, upward pressure is put on the deutsche mark within the EMS, and Germany's economy receives a differential boost. Furthermore, the asymmetry in output will be aggravated by the asymmetry in the wealth effects noted above, which point to a further tightening of aggregate demand in the United States and a further expansion in Germany. These predictions are consistent with what we have observed over the last year.

Growth Effects

A second worry has been that the reduction in investment in the OECD and the developing countries will reduce growth in the medium run in both regions. This worry is justified for the developing countries, but not for the industrial countries.

With respect to the developing countries, we have already discussed the tight link between net resource transfers from abroad and domestic investment. As long as some of the increase in capital flows to EESU comes at the expense of resource transfers to these countries, which appears inevitable, investment and growth will be direct casualties. Let us assume, for example, that additional capital flows to EESU are $55 billion, as in scenario II in table 3.7. The market's implicit forecast of the reduction in resource transfers to the developing countries amounts then to 0.8 percent of their GDP, and the reduction in investment is 0.6 percent of their GDP.

However, since the capital flows to EESU will come from the OECD area, the growth consequences for the industrial countries are quite different. It is true that, given lower domestic investment, domestic output will expand at a slower rate. But the redirection of investment from the OECD area to EESU is a reflection of the availability of higher-yielding opportunities in EESU. Consequently, national income in the OECD countries should grow faster, once net factor payments from abroad are taken into account. In other words, while gross *domestic* product is likely to grow slower, gross *national* product will grow faster. Since the latter is a more accurate indicator of national well-being, OECD policymakers have little reason to worry about the growth consequences for their own countries of EESU transformation. In this respect, the effects are symmetric across all OECD countries. The United States will benefit also, although possibly less than some of the European countries, which will be the primary suppliers of capital to EESU.

Although the growth effect is positive for the OECD area, its importance should not be exaggerated. A $55 billion net increase in flows to EESU (scenario II) amounts to just 0.4 percent of combined OECD GNP. Even if the real yield differential on this were a full 10 percentage points, OECD growth would be spurred by only 0.04 percentage points (0.4 × 0.10).

Income-Distributional Effects

Internal distributional considerations may detract from the rosy scenario sketched above for the OECD countries. The distributional implications are perhaps sharpest for low-skilled labor. Capital owners, professionals, and skilled workers, being on the whole internationally mobile, are well placed to take advantage of the new opportunities opened up by the integration of EESU. The gains indicated above will accrue primarily to these groups. Most workers, and low-skilled workers in particular, are not mobile, and are therefore likely to suffer as production facilities expand abroad and not at home. However, for the same reason noted above, we should not overstate the quantitative importance of these distributional effects.

Conclusions

We have argued in this chapter that transformation in Eastern Europe and the Soviet Union is likely to result in modest capital flows from the developed countries over the next few years. Other things equal, these transfers will affect both interest rates in international capital markets and the amount of capital available to the developing countries. In particular, we have shown that there is a trade-off between the magnitude of the effects on each of these. The key questions then are how large the flows to EESU will be, what the effects on interest rates and developing countries will be, and what the overall implications are for different regions of the global economy. For the first two of these questions, we have identified what we believe to be the relevant range of likely outcomes, together with an intermediate scenario that we find plausible. As discussed at the outset, any such calculations necessarily rely on a host of assumptions, and the resulting estimates should be treated accordingly.

We believe that annual capital flows to the region will be modest in the near term—from a low of $30 billion to at most $90 billion. An intermediate figure of $55 billion appears to us quite plausible. These figures include flows to the Soviet Union and to the former East Germany. By far the largest component and the most uncertain is capital flows associated with German unification. In particular, it is unclear how much of the costs of reconstruction will be financed internally by the former West Germany.

Other things equal, increased transfers to EESU either must be offset by reduced transfers to developing countries, or must raise interest rates in international capital markets, to the extent that total demand for resources from the industrial countries increases. Our empirical estimates suggest that industrial-country saving is relatively unresponsive to interest rate changes, while the responsiveness of investment is relatively low. This implies that interest rates must rise substantially to generate additional resources for any increase in the total transfer from developed countries. In other words, there is a steep trade-off between how much interest rates or transfers to developing countries must adjust in response to increased capital flows to the East.

Our empirical estimates also suggest that investment in the developing countries is closely related to the size of the resource transfer they receive. More than 75 cents of each dollar (net) received goes to investment expenditures. Therefore, reductions in net resource transfers to the developing countries would have worrisome consequences for capital accumulation and for the future growth prospects for these countries.

Our estimates imply ranges for the magnitude of the impact, based on whether capital flows to the region are $30 billion or $90 billion. In particular, real interest rates could rise by 1 to 3 percentage points if there is no offsetting reduction in transfers to the developing countries. Alternatively, for interest rates to remain the same, net transfers to the developing countries would have to be cut by the amount of transfers to EESU, resulting in reductions in developing-country investment amounting to 0.8 percent to 2.3 percent of their GDP. These are the lower and upper bounds. However, we note that real interest rates have already risen by about 1 percentage point in response to developments in the region. Our estimates suggest that this rise is consistent with a $30 billion transfer to EESU, with no offsetting reduction in transfers to the developing countries. However, focusing on the scenario that we believe most plausible (a transfer to EESU of about $55 billion per year), the 1-percentage-point rise in interest rates suggests that transfers to developing countries will fall by some $25 billion during 1991, implying a reduction of about 0.6 percent of their GDP in their investment.

Finally, we discussed the regional implications of higher interest rates and a reduced transfer to the developing countries. Because the developing countries are net debtors in the aggregate, as a group they are clearly hurt by these developments. Because the industrial countries are net creditors in the aggregate, as a group they benefit from higher interest rates as well as from an expanded set of investment opportunities. However, within each of these groups the losses or the gains are distributed unequally. In particular, the net impact for the United States—a net debtor—may be recessionary, whereas the impact is clearly expansionary for Germany. Also, higher interest rates will tend to reduce investment on developed-country soil as resources are shifted toward more profitable investment in the transforming EESU. To the extent that labor is less mobile than capital, workers in the developed countries stand to lose as production facilities expand abroad instead of at home.

4 Conclusions and Policy Implications

This study has analyzed the consequences of the economic transition in Eastern Europe and the Soviet Union (EESU) for the global economy, focusing on the implications for international trade, capital flows, and macroeconomic performance. In this final chapter, we summarize and integrate our conclusions and draw policy implications for Europe, the United States, Japan, and the developing countries.

Our analysis necessarily relies on assumptions about what the transition in EESU will mean, and about how the rest of the world will respond. Any set of assumptions about these very uncertain events is, of course, highly speculative. As discussed in chapter 1, successful transitions will entail a combination of sensible macroeconomic policies, price reform, and institutional developments, such as laws to protect private property, privatization of state-owned enterprises, and creation of financial intermediaries. The countries of the region will need to rebuild their severely depleted capital stocks and to adopt modern, more efficient technologies.

The political situations and economic starting points in individual countries differ markedly, and there is no simple recipe for success. We do not underestimate the difficulties involved in a successful transition to a market economy. However, our objective is to examine the potential implications of transition, and these will be greater the more successful the transformation turns out to be.

Thus, our approach has been to specify a "full catch-up" scenario in which transition proceeds smoothly in two senses. First, countries in the region become "like" other developed market economies, perhaps over the next two decades. Second, the transition is not blocked by protectionist or restrictive policies in the rest of the world. We also discussed what we believe to be more realistic scenarios, based in part on our summary of individual countries in the region. Although the assumption of full catch-up is unreasonably optimistic—as we will discuss further below—we believe it provides a useful benchmark for

111

identifying the likely implications of transition and highlighting the potential tensions and policy issues that will emerge. We have also tried to present enough background information so that the interested reader can construct alternative scenarios for comparison. In the remainder of this chapter, we summarize our major conclusions and identify some policy dilemmas for the industrialized countries of the West.

Much of our discussion in the preceding chapters has focused on the differential impacts on the United States, the European Community, and the developing countries. As we have stressed above and will again in this chapter, the effects will be felt differently by different groups of countries. But these asymmetries should not cloud the fact that the economic opening of EESU is a source of benefit for the world economy as a whole. This is true on at least two accounts. First, the expansion of trade to include EESU provides the world economy with the potential to reap the benefits of greater specialization. Second, the emergence of new, high-yielding investment opportunities in EESU enhances the prospects for worldwide growth and prosperity.

How significant are these overall effects likely to be? We can form a rough idea by considering that, according to our estimates, the transition in EESU could enlarge world trade by 2 percent to 3 percent in the medium run (and perhaps by as much as 15 percent in the long run). It could lead to annual (net) capital flows to the region of as much as $90 billion over the next five years, which is more than 2 percent of global investment (and 3 percent of OECD investment). Hence the overall global impact is perhaps not huge, but neither is it insignificant.

Trade Implications

The countries of Eastern Europe are small relative to the world economy when considered individually, but potentially sizable when taken as a group. This is even more true if the Soviet Union is included. Eastern Europe's population is roughly 40 percent of that of the European Community. At present, however, the combined income of the region is less than 20 percent of that in the Community. The Soviet population is nearly nine-tenths the EC total, but recent estimates put its per capita income even lower than the average in Eastern Europe.

A successful economic transition that raised these per capita income levels to the average enjoyed in the European Community, for example, would substantially increase the region's global economic importance. Eastern Europe's GNP could rise from just 3 percent of world GNP to over 6 percent. Including the Soviet Union, the region's total production could rise from less than 10 percent of world output to over 20 percent.

Our analysis suggests that the combined region could ultimately account for almost a quarter (23 percent) of total world exports, compared with less than 10 percent currently. This is proportionately smaller than the gains achieved by the East Asian NICs, but the absolute increase would be much larger. We would not expect the countries in the region to run very large trade deficits (see the discussion in the next section). Over the long run, both export and import volumes should expand commensurately. Among the region's economies, only Poland and Yugoslavia are markedly less open to foreign trade than the norm among market-oriented economies. Therefore, most of the impact on global trade volumes would come as a result of the closing of the gap in living standards between Eastern and Western Europe. The impact of increased openness to trade arising from economic liberalization is in itself likely to be small, amounting to an expansion of world trade by 2 percent to 3 percent. And since the catching-up process will be a lengthy one, the immediate impact will not be large in the aggregate, and the world economy will have plenty of time to adjust itself to the eventual expansion of trade.

The picture looks somewhat different when we turn to the potential impact of the transition on specific markets. Our analysis, based on the interwar trade patterns of the region (in particular the late 1920s) as well as the postwar experience of several comparator countries, suggests that liberalization will result in a major reorientation of Eastern European and Soviet trade toward Western markets and away from each other. We expect bilateral trade between Eastern Europe and the Soviet Union to come down sharply; intra–Eastern European trade will suffer much less and may even increase.

In quantitative terms, the magnitude of the impact will be greatest by far on Western Europe, and within Western Europe on Germany. Our estimates are that EESU could account for more than a quarter (27 percent to 28 percent) of EC trade in the long run, up from 4 percent to

5 percent presently. Even in the absence of any catch-up in per capita incomes (which is our medium-run scenario), the share of EESU in EC trade would triple to 12 percent. The implied trade with Germany is even larger. These calculations assume that EESU will have unhindered access to EC markets. But in fact it is difficult to believe that the market penetration levels in Europe implied by our estimates could be reached without engendering a protectionist backlash within the Community, in the form of antidumping actions or quantitative restrictions in specific sectors.

There is an alternative scenario. It is possible that in the future a healthy, market-oriented, and growing Soviet economy will present an outlet for the exports of Eastern European countries, which in turn will offer their markets to Soviet exports. Forty-five years of intra–EESU trade has created complementarities in production that will not disappear overnight. Our statistical analysis may well have underestimated the potential trade pull of this giant economy.

However, there are also strong arguments against this alternative scenario. Although it is dangerous to predict the form that the region's politics will take in the future, current developments in the Soviet Union are not encouraging with respect to the speed and extent of market-oriented reform. Forced to make a bet, we would guess that the Soviet economy will stagnate, if not deteriorate further, over the next few years. Production complementarities notwithstanding, the Eastern European countries will have to look for markets elsewhere. And as Poland and Hungary have demonstrated with their trade performance during 1990, a major geographical redirection of trade can take place very quickly indeed.

Hence, integrating EESU into the European trading system will be a major challenge of the 1990s. For the prosperity of the world economy, it will be important to achieve this integration without multiplying the use of those protectionist instruments and hierarchies of preference that are already in place. The dangerous temptation in the European Community will be to incorporate the Eastern European countries into the EC trading system by creating a new level of preferences, and simply pushing other groups of countries (e.g., the nonassociated developing countries, the Mediterranean countries, or the African, Caribbean, and Pacific countries, and possibly the United States and Japan as well) one rung down the ladder of market access. If this temptation is not avoided, the trade gains of EESU will come directly at the expense of the developing countries, which are least able to retaliate against EC measures directed against them. Reduced access to developed-country markets would erode the developing countries' ability to revive growth after a decade of poor economic performance and (in many countries) falling per capita incomes. It would also hinder their ability to meet external debt obligations and increase pressures for additional debt reduction, especially if the Eastern European debtors secure favorable debt agreements with their Western creditors (as Poland already has).

Increased trade with Eastern Europe also has potentially important implications for agricultural policies in Western Europe. Maintaining the Common Agricultural Policy (CAP), which has long been a centerpiece of the European Community, is likely to prove incompatible with the extension of free trade between EC member countries and the Eastern European countries. Such is the agricultural trade potential of Hungary, Poland, and Romania that expanding trade with these countries, in the absence of a serious reform of the CAP, would result in either an explosion in the already rapidly rising budgetary cost of the CAP or the erection of an extensive network of quantitative restrictions on agricultural imports from EESU. It would be preferable to substantially reduce price supports and export subsidies within the CAP. By doing so soon, the Community would be killing two birds with one stone: it would reduce trade tensions with the United States and other agricultural exporters and help bring the current round of multilateral trade negotiations to a conclusion, and it would ameliorate the inevitable crisis that lies around the corner as a result of the market-oriented reforms in EESU.

More generally, who are the likely winners and losers from expanding trade flows to and from the East? For the industrialized countries, EESU will be a market for exports as well as a source of imports. Consumers and producers as a whole will benefit from this mutual expansion of trade, tensions in sensitive sectors notwithstanding. For the developing countries, on the other hand, the impact threatens to be negative. In all likelihood, the initial phase of EESU exports will be based on agricultural commodities and on products where labor-cost advantages play an important role. Exports of the latter will compete head-on with labor-intensive manufactures presently exported by the developing countries. In commodities like textiles, clothing, footwear, steel, and (potentially) consumer electronics, developing countries will face new competitors with greater geographical proximity to European markets and greater cultural and political ties to the importers. The Polish experience of 1990 clearly shows that establishing a relatively undervalued exchange rate enables Eastern European producers to compete with other suppliers.

Meanwhile, since capital goods will be the predominant EESU import, the developing countries will not be able to avail themselves of these new markets as much as will the industrialized countries. The market-share and terms-of-trade consequences are likely to be particularly adverse for the middle-income developing countries, and potentially for the Southern European countries as well.

Here too there is an alternative scenario. The economies of Eastern Europe have high levels of human capital, as reflected in their educational attainment and the composition of their work forces. If this human capital can form the basis for comparative advantage in skill-intensive manufactures, the adverse effect on developing-country exports could turn out to be limited. As we argued in chapter 2, however, the skill potential of the region needs to be "validated" by inflows of physical capital and transfers of Western technology before it can exert a determining influence on EESU exports. In the absence of large-scale capital inflows, the countries of the region are likely to make their entrance into the world economy as low-cost producers of relatively standardized and labor-intensive products.

Macroeconomic Implications

If Eastern Europe and the Soviet Union are to raise their living standards to levels enjoyed in the developed market economies, the region as a whole will require massive investments in physical capital. However, it is extremely unrealistic to assume that much of the financing for these investments will come from the developed market economies—with the exception of financing for German unification. There are no evident sources for capital flows sufficient to finance large external deficits—and in particular there are no evident sources for large grants. Loans would exacerbate the already-worrisome external debt difficulties of several countries in the region. Further, the experience of those countries furthest along in implementing market-oriented policies has been a sharp improvement in their hard-currency external balances. Poland has been running substantial trade surpluses. Most of the needed investments to rebuild physical capital stocks will have to be financed internally. Therefore, regional capital requirements calculated using needs-based approaches (i.e., targeting a specific growth rate or the equalization of capital-labor ratios with those prevailing in the West) do not provide a useful approach for estimating likely capital flows to the region.

Focusing on the potential sources of funds, we estimate that the likely magnitude of inflows to the region will be relatively small: in the range of $30 billion to $90 billion (net) per year for the next five years, the greater part of which will be allocated to eastern Germany. The two major sources of uncertainty are the cost of German unification and further developments in the Soviet economy. Where we will end up in this range depends primarily on these two factors.

These modest capital flow estimates are consistent with our assessments of small trade deficits in the region over the next few years. Also, these magnitudes are comparable to the assistance Western Europe received for reconstruction through the Marshall Plan. Countries that successfully reduce the extreme uncertainty about future economic performance may attract substantially greater capital inflows down the road, in the form of foreign direct investment.

Our assessment of the likely private capital flows over the next five years are based in part on a survey of private investors. Our 54 respondents revealed considerable interest in the region. They expect to triple or quadruple the share of the region in their investment portfolios over the next five years. However, this does not translate into large inflows, because the base is so low to begin with: even with this increase, our respondents anticipate that the shares of Eastern Europe and Soviet Union, separately, will remain considerably below 2 percent of their total foreign investments. Hungary and eastern Germany are judged to present the most attractive investment climates, with Czechoslovakia and Poland distant followers. Political and economic uncertainty, lack of legal protection for private property, and concerns over the ability to repatriate profits are all perceived to be major obstacles to investment. The potential presented by new and expanding markets and the need to beat out competitors are cited as the main attractions of going in. Interestingly, foreign investors do not perceive low labor costs, high labor skills, or proximity to the EC market to be major attractions.

Given our range of likely capital flows into the region, what are the major implications for the rest of the world? Our econometric evidence suggests two important elements that go into answering this question. First, saving in the industrial world is relatively insensitive to changes in interest rates. Second, world interest rates are highly sensitive to changes in investment demand. Thus, any net increase in investment demand for capital would tend to push interest rates up considerably. Capital flows from the developed economies to finance investments in EESU can come either through a reduction in domestic investment (net of saving), or from a reduction in capital flows to the developing countries. If capital flows to the developing countries are held constant, an increase in flows to EESU can come about only as a result of an increase in world interest rates, which serves to crowd out *domestic* investment in the developed economies. The implication is that there is a trade-off—and a fairly steep one—between the effect on world interest rates and the effect on resource transfers to the developing countries.

If, at one extreme, none of the increase in capital flows to EESU comes at the expense of the developing countries, we estimate that the effect on world interest rates would be a rise of between roughly 1 and 3 percentage points, with the low and high estimates corresponding, respectively, to the low and high ends of the capital flows range. In this case, the full transfer to EESU ($30 billion to $90 billion, depending on the scenario) would come out of domestic investment in the developed countries). If, on the other hand, all of the increase comes at the expense of the developing countries, so that there is no net increase in the global demand for resources, the reduction in net transfers to the developing countries would be in the range of 1.0 percent to 3.0 percent of developing-country income, resulting in a drop in investment in that group of countries of 0.8 percent to 2.3 percent of their GDP. The likely scenario lies somewhere in between these two extremes: the transfer of resources to EESU will be accommodated partly by an increase in world interest rates, and partly by a reduction in transfers to the developing countries.

However, it is important to point out that the implied increases in interest rates may already have occurred. To the extent that investors are forward-looking and quickly respond to new information about demands for and supplies of resources, most of the interest rate effects should have occurred soon after the revolutions of 1989, when the possibility of market-oriented reform in the region became clear. Large additional changes in interest rates are likely only in the event of major new information about opportunities in the region. And it is certainly possible that that new information would suggest a reduction—not a further expansion—in such opportunities.

Interest rates indeed rose worldwide in 1989–90 as the revolutions in Eastern Europe started to unfold. We can attribute about 100 basis points of this rise directly to the "news" about EESU. Let us assume that capital markets correctly foresaw the magnitude of the net increase in global demand for resources, as reflected in this interest rate rise. Suppose also that annual capital flows to EESU turn out to be in the middle of our range, that is, about $55 billion. The implication, given the trade-off we have estimated between interest rates and capital transfers, is that markets predicted that about $25 billion of these capital flows would come at the expense of the developing countries (and $30 billion at the expense of investment in the industrial countries). If capital flows to EESU end up higher, the implied reduction in flows to developing countries will be commensurately larger.

From the standpoint of the developing countries, then, the effects are clear. They face the combined effects of an increase in global interest rates and a reduction in net resource transfers. It should be stressed that these have independent and cumulative effects on the welfare of poor countries. The increase in interest rates has a direct negative wealth effect, as these countries are large net debtors to the rest of the world. If net (floating-rate) debt stands at around 30 percent of the developing countries' GDP on average, the increase in interest rates has reduced real income in these countries by 0.3 percent already. The reduction in net resource transfers magnifies this effect by causing investment to fall. Since developing countries are credit-constrained, their investment levels are already too low from the standpoint of economic welfare. The reduction in external inflows will only aggravate the situation.

With respect to the industrialized countries, we think many of the concerns that are typically raised are unfounded. These concerns center mainly around the implications of higher interest rates. However, if we look at the industrialized countries in aggregate, the increase in interest rates brings a lot of good news, and little bad news. First, these countries as a group are net creditors and will therefore receive a positive wealth transfer from the rest of the world as interest rates rise. Second, for the OECD region as a whole, the decrease in domestic investment demand will be modest. Further, it will essentially be offset by an equivalent increase in net exports since little change in domestic saving can be expected, leaving aggregate demand unaffected. In other words, capital equipment that was previously invested at home will now be exported to EESU; there will be no recessionary impulse on average. The wealth effect noted above, meanwhile, will generate an expansionary impulse. The net effect of increased interest rates need not be a reduction in aggregate demand, and therefore the interest rate shock need not be recessionary.

Nor do we find the concern about the longer-run growth consequences of reduced domestic investment in the developed countries entirely justified. It is true that a reduction in domestic investment will lower the growth rate of gross domestic product. However, the growth rate of gross *national* product should increase. Domestic investors will not divert their capital eastward unless the returns to investment in EESU are expected to be higher than on comparably risky investments at home. Once net factor payments from abroad are taken into account, then, national income should increase more quickly, thanks to the high-yielding opportunities in EESU.

Although the picture looks rosy for the industrial countries as a whole, these effects are unlikely to work uniformly within the group. Most notably, the situations of the United States and the European Community are quite different. The United States is a net debtor, and in this respect stands to lose from an increase in interest rates. There is also no reason to expect that the counteracting effect of net exports on aggregate demand will be felt equally in the United States and the European Community. In fact, as our trade predictions suggest strongly, EESU's trade will be dominated by the Western European countries. The main beneficiaries of the region's capital rehabilitation and import expansion, therefore, will also be the Western European countries. We may expect Western Europe to end up with an expansionary impulse, as the increase in its net exports will (on impact) outstrip the reduction in domestic investment demand. This is already clear in Germany's case: the magnitude of the transfers to eastern Germany is heating up the economy and forcing the federal government to undertake restrictive demand policies. Another indication of the same phenomenon is the appreciation of the European currencies against the dollar during 1990. This appreciation reflected the markets' belief that the integration of EESU will have more favorable effects on the trade balance of Western Europe than on that of the United States.

Thus there will be a certain asymmetry in the macroeconomic repercussions of EESU transformation upon the United States and Western Europe. In the United States, negative effects from increased interest rates are likely to dominate and may make the recovery from the 1990–91 recession more difficult. In Western Europe, both the trade balance and the interest rate effects will tend to be expansionary.

A similar asymmetry operates within Europe, between Germany and some of the other members of the European Community. Countries such as Belgium and Italy have high levels of public debt, and for them the interest rate shock does not come as good news. Similarly, the net trade impact will not be as significant and positive for the United Kingdom, say, as it will for Germany. Therefore the German economy will experience a considerably more expansionary stimulus than the other members of the Community. For some members, the net impact on aggregate demand could even be negative (as in the case of the United States).

This asymmetry suggests that policymakers will have contradictory goals, not only in the United States and the European Community, but within the Community as well, with Germany's interests potentially conflicting with those of the other members. Consequently, policy coordination may prove difficult to achieve, and a certain amount of tension in Germany's external economic relations will be unavoidable. Such tensions were already evident in February 1991, when the Bundesbank pushed its interest rate up at the same time that the Federal Reserve was trying to push US interest rates down. US officials complained that the German authorities were not being cooperative enough. The Germans, for their part, felt that the United States was not sensitive enough to the huge burden of reconstructing eastern Germany.

The last example points to what is perhaps one of the most important potential implications of Eastern European integration, namely, German preoccupation with domestic matters at the expense of international cooperation. Such is the scope of the internal social, political, and economic challenges raised by German unification that it should not be surprising if German policymaking becomes governed by domestic concerns, and appears less responsive to international demands and obligations. For any country but one of Germany's size and importance to the world economy, the external consequences may not have been significant. But if Germany should turn inward, the damage done to the progress of European Economic and Monetary Union (EMU) and international cooperation in general could be tremendous. So far, there is little to suggest that a decisive shift of this sort is in the offing. But there have been several signs of small changes in emphasis:

- In the immediate aftermath of the economic unification of the two Germanys, the Bundesbank began to blow cool air on the European Commission's advocacy of a speeded-up transition to monetary union. The difficulties being experienced in eastern Germany are being used by the Bundesbank to caution against a "premature" move to a common currency within the European Monetary System.
- Some of the military allies in the 1991 Gulf war—especially the United Kingdom—have expressed doubts as to whether Germany has lived up to its international obligations and has made sufficient resources available to the nations involved in the fighting. This is a difficult issue within Germany, given the existing budgetary burden of unification.
- As mentioned above, the Bundesbank raised its key interest rate in February 1991, while the Federal Reserve was busy trying to lower US rates. US policymakers made it clear that the Bundesbank's move was not a helpful one to the objective of easing the recession in the United States and elsewhere.

The danger is that such episodes could multiply and progressively distance Germany both from her EC partners and from the United States.

For Japan, the direct economic effects of transformation in EESU will tend to be small but uniformly positive. Japan will benefit both from the redirection of trade in EESU and from the wealth effect of the interest rate shock. Japan will share—on a smaller scale—all the benefits that will accrue to Germany, without feeling any of the negative effects. Our estimates predict that EESU will run "structural" trade deficits with Japan, so that import penetration issues are unlikely to arise in sensitive sectors of the Japanese economy. Furthermore, unlike Western Europe, Japan will not face the threat of labor emigration from EESU if the economies of the region do not recover soon.

Lest one think, however, that this is one area that will not aggravate US–Japan and EC–Japan tensions, it is possible to construct an argument to the contrary. As noted above, Japan will be a clear, if small, winner from the integration of EESU into the world economy. At the same time, in view of Japan's geographical distance from Eastern Europe, its lack of historical ties, and its seemingly inherent reluctance to play a leading international role, Japan will probably feel little inclination to contribute much resources to reconstruction there.[1] (The situation may be different with respect to the reconstruction of Soviet Union.) It is possible that this will intensify the ongoing debate about burdensharing in the world economy and Japan's appropriate global role. To avoid tensions, Japan will have to take a more active role in the provision of international public goods: open markets for trade, public capital for EESU reconstruction, and international macroeconomic policy cooperation.

Policy Dilemmas

Internal reforms are by far the most important determinant of whether market-oriented transformations will succeed in Eastern Europe and the Soviet Union, but the policy response of the West can help or hinder the likelihood of success. The most supportive environment would include open markets for trade and foreign assistance—including some financial assistance, debt relief for some countries, transfer of technology, and technical assistance in a wide range of areas. In our view, the road is likely to be especially rocky for trade policy issues. But on both the trade and the macroeconomic fronts, a major concern should be that policymakers in the developed countries do not ease the domestic burden of supporting transition in the East by shifting the costs to the developing countries.

---

1. As this study went to press, Japanese policymakers were complaining about the debt reduction plan offered to Poland, and may withhold a $500 million loan they had previously promised.

We conclude our discussion by raising two policy dilemmas that industrial-country policymakers face as a result of the ongoing reforms in Eastern Europe and the Soviet Union. The first is related to the trade-off between the magnitude of capital flows to EESU and the increased trade competition that will eventually result from this investment. As we suggested in chapter 2, whether EESU end up exporting skill-intensive products (and therefore compete with the industrial countries) or labor-intensive products (and therefore compete with the developing countries) depends in large part on the extent and form of capital flows that will be forthcoming. The high levels of human and technical skills that EESU no doubt possess need to be unlocked by complementary capital flows, which would provide not only resources but also up-to-date technology. Might it not be more in the industrial countries' interest to deny them such flows, so as to make EESU exports displace developing-country producers rather than their own?

For the Western European countries, where the dilemma is sharpest, it is also moderated by other considerations arising out of self-interest. The gap between East and West can be closed either by capital flows from the West or by labor migration from the East. If Western Europe does not provide the capital, it may well end up with a major labor migration problem on its hands. Further, if Europeans do not assist in the recovery of the Soviet Union, they will soon be at the receiving end of a larger trade diversion by the Eastern European countries. On both accounts, generous capital flows to the East—including debt reduction and technical assistance—make sense for Western Europe.

The second dilemma has to do with burdenshifting to the developing countries. The industrial countries, and the European Community in particular, can alleviate the impact of expanded imports from EESU by erecting higher barriers against developing-country exports. Similarly, they can cushion the global interest rate impact by reducing resource transfers to the developing countries. In both areas, the industrial countries have the opportunity to shift some of the cost of EESU integration onto the developing countries. Since much of the developing world is already engulfed in a serious economic crisis, the potential negative impact could be significant. It is in the interest of the world economy that the dilemma not be resolved by shifting the adjustment burden to those countries least able to support it.

A Estimation of the Geographical Composition of Trade of Eastern Europe and the Soviet Union

The estimation of the posttransition geographical composition of EESU trade following the transition to market economies is based on the trade patterns of a group of six comparator countries: Austria, Finland, Germany, Italy, Portugal, and Spain. The trade partners included are the United States; Japan, Korea, and Taiwan (as a group); Austria; Belgium and Luxembourg (together); Denmark; Finland; France; Germany; Greece; Italy; the Netherlands; Norway; Portugal; Spain; Sweden; Switzerland; the United Kingdom; China; India, Burma, and Sri Lanka (as a group); Turkey; Egypt; Iran; Iraq; Libya; Argentina; and Brazil; as well as the six Eastern European countries (omitting East Germany) and the Soviet Union. Trade data for 1928 are taken from the League of Nations (1942). The groupings of some of the countries reflect those in the League of Nations' prewar trade matrix.

We ran regressions using the 1989 shares of these partners in the comparator countries' trade flows as the dependent variable. The independent variables were the corresponding 1928 import or export shares and dummies for each of the partners. We ran one regression each for import and export shares. The form of the regression is as follows:

(A.1) $M89_{ij}$ = constant
          $+ \alpha^m M28_{ij} + \Sigma_j \beta_j{}^m PARTNER_j + \gamma^m SU + \delta^m EE + \epsilon^m$

(A.2) $X89_{ij}$ = constant $+ \alpha^x X28_{ij} + \Sigma_j \beta_j{}^x PARTNER_j + \gamma^x SU + \delta^x EE + \epsilon^x$

where $M89_{ij}$ is the share of partner j in comparator i's imports in 1989, $M28_{ij}$ is the corresponding share for 1928, $PARTNER_j$ is a dummy for each of the (Western) partners, SU is the Soviet Union dummy, EE is the Eastern Europe dummy, and ϵ^m is a random error term. The second equation is the corresponding one for exports. All dummies with a t-statistic less than one were dropped. Note that we combined dummies

TABLE A.1   Import share regression results[a]

Variable	Estimated coefficient	t-statistic
Constant	0.867E-02	3.22
M28[b]	0.266	5.29
United States dummy	0.153E-01	1.22
Japan-Korea-Taiwan dummy	0.529E-01	4.82
Belgium-Luxembourg dummy	0.222E-01	2.02
France dummy	0.720E-01	6.35
Germany dummy	0.169	11.66
Italy dummy	0.690E-01	5.77
Netherlands dummy	0.335E-01	3.06
Spain dummy	0.300E-01	2.51
Soviet Union dummy	0.197E-01	1.80
EE6 dummy	−0.941E-02	−1.87

Adjusted R-squared = 0.71
Number of observations = 192

a. See text for methodology.
b. Partner-country import share in 1928.

for the six Eastern European countries, since the estimated coefficients for individual countries in the region were very close in value. EESU therefore enters the regressions with two dummies: one just for the Soviet Union, and one for the other six countries.

The results of the regression predict the 1989 import and export shares of countries with their trading partners (see tables A.1 and A.2). For example, the estimated share of country i's imports coming from the United States would be:

$$0.00867 + [0.26649(M28_{iUS})] + 0.01528,$$

where $M28_{iUS}$ is the share of the United States in country i's imports. As mentioned in the text, however, predictions made in this way would overstate EESU trade with the West. Had EESU not separated them-

TABLE A.2   Export share regression results[a]

Variable	Estimated coefficient	t-statistic
Constant	0.691E-02	2.83
X28[b]	0.461	11.02
United States dummy	0.243E-01	2.40
Japan-Korea-Taiwan dummy	0.157E-01	1.59
Belgium-Luxembourg dummy	0.113E-01	1.15
France dummy	0.653E-01	6.17
Germany dummy	0.110	9.31
Italy dummy	0.438E-01	4.05
Netherlands dummy	0.184E-01	1.85
Spain dummy	0.352E-01	3.27
Soviet Union dummy	0.233E-01	2.37
EE6 dummy	−0.109E-01	−2.40

Adjusted R-squared = 0.73
Number of observations = 192

a. See text for methodology.
b. Partner-country export share in 1928.

selves from the international trading community, the comparator countries would have traded more with EESU and less with the West. Therefore, the comparator countries' observed trade with the West are biased upward as predictors of EESU trade with the West. We have to allow for this, since presumably this bias will be corrected once EESU liberalize.

To do that, we use our results with respect to the EESU partner dummies. We assume that dropping the EESU dummies would predict what the partner countries' trade would have been if EESU had not separated themselves. In other words, the regressions predict country i's current import shares from Bulgaria (for example) to equal:

$$0.00867 + [0.26649(M28_{iB})] - 0.00941,$$

where $M28_{iB}$ is the 1928 share. Under the counterfactual supposition that Bulgaria had never become socialist, the prediction would be:

$$0.00867 + [0.26649(M28_{iB})],$$

which is greater. Note that the estimated coefficient for the Soviet Union dummy is positive, indicating that the Soviet Union, unlike the Eastern European countries, is trading more with the West now than its trade in 1928 would indicate. We return to this issue below.

Presumably, if we estimated the import shares of all trading partners according to the regression, the shares would sum to unity. If we drop the EESU dummies to determine what their shares would have been absent socialism, these shares now add up to $1 - 0.01974 + [6(0.00941)]$ = 1.03672. We assume that all countries were affected by the trade diversion by the same proportion. So, to get our revised estimate of import shares, we divide the previous share estimates by 1.03672. The same procedure is followed to estimate export shares.

As mentioned in the text, a second adjustment was undertaken to correct for the special circumstances of the Soviet economy in 1928. The assumption made was that the Soviet Union would exert an influence on the trade of each of the individual Eastern European countries similar to that exerted by the other EE6 countries. Therefore, we constructed a "proportionality coefficient" for each of the EE6 countries, equal to the ratio of global Soviet trade in our medium-run scenario to the corresponding number for the EE6 countries (excluding the home country). This coefficient was multiplied by the EE6 trade share of each country to get the revised trade share for the Soviet Union. All trade shares were then scaled down proportionately, to sum to 100 percent.

Predictions of the geographical composition of trade for each of the Eastern European countries and the Soviet Union are presented in tables A.3 through A.9.

TABLE A.3   **Bulgaria: geographical composition of trade by individual partner country, 1928, 1989, and predicted** (percentages of total)

Country	Imports			Exports		
	1928	1989	Predicted	1928	1989	Predicted
United States	2.33	1.54	2.64	1.32	0.87	3.27
Japan-Korea-Taiwan	0.00	1.39	5.39	0.00	0.59	1.99
Austria	8.14	1.33	2.66	14.47	0.49	6.47
Belgium-Luxembourg	3.49	0.55	3.51	3.95	0.21	3.20
Denmark	0.00	0.21	0.76	0.00	0.05	0.61
Finland	0.00	0.29	0.76	0.00	0.17	0.61
France	8.14	1.29	8.96	6.58	0.98	9.01
Germany	20.93	6.67	20.39	27.63	2.31	21.44
Greece	1.16	0.40	1.03	7.89	0.81	3.80
Italy	15.12	2.31	10.32	11.84	1.58	9.25
Netherlands	2.33	0.72	4.24	3.95	0.52	3.82
Norway	0.00	0.04	0.76	0.00	0.02	0.61
Portugal	0.00	0.05	0.76	0.00	0.05	0.61
Spain	0.00	0.25	3.39	0.00	0.54	3.70
Sweden	1.16	0.53	1.03	0.00	0.15	0.61
Switzerland	2.33	1.32	1.30	1.32	0.19	1.14
United Kingdom	10.47	1.21	3.20	2.63	0.74	1.67
China	0.00	0.50	0.76	0.00	1.32	0.61
India–Burma–Sri Lanka	0.00	0.34	0.76	0.00	1.55	0.61
Turkey	2.33	0.23	1.30	5.26	0.32	2.74
Egypt	1.16	0.06	1.03	1.32	0.25	1.14
Iran	0.00	0.00	0.76	0.00	0.00	0.61
Iraq	0.00	0.00	0.76	0.00	0.00	0.61
Libya	0.00	1.41	0.76	0.00	1.30	0.61
Argentina	0.00	0.65	0.76	0.00	0.09	0.61
Brazil	0.00	0.42	0.76	0.00	0.00	0.61
Czechoslovakia	10.47	4.34	3.20	2.63	4.41	1.67
Hungary	2.33	0.91	1.30	2.63	1.59	1.67
Poland	1.16	2.24	1.03	3.95	2.41	2.21
Romania	5.81	2.93	2.11	2.63	6.91	1.67
Soviet Union	0.00	57.39	10.05	0.00	58.10	9.07
Yugoslavia	1.16	1.12	1.03	0.00	2.08	0.61
Totals	100.00	92.61	97.46	100.00	90.58	96.84

Sources: Trade figures for 1928 are from League of Nations (1942). Figures for 1989 are from International Monetary Fund (1990a).

TABLE   A.4   Czechoslovakia: geographical composition of trade by
individual partner country, 1928, 1989, and predicted
(percentages of total)

Country	Imports			Exports		
	1928	1989	Predicted	1928	1989	Predicted
United States	5.94	0.32	3.48	5.56	0.56	4.73
Japan-Korea-Taiwan	0.10	0.35	5.42	0.28	0.90	1.99
Austria	7.40	2.00	2.49	14.70	2.67	6.22
Belgium-Luxembourg	1.56	0.52	3.07	0.75	0.60	1.81
Denmark	0.21	0.34	0.81	1.32	0.46	1.08
Finland	0.00	0.49	0.76	0.47	0.70	0.76
France	4.27	1.37	8.07	1.32	1.58	6.52
Germany	38.65	8.63	24.55	26.77	7.79	20.00
Greece	0.31	0.20	0.83	0.66	0.59	0.83
Italy	3.33	1.60	7.58	3.77	2.24	5.67
Netherlands	1.46	0.99	4.04	1.79	1.12	2.80
Norway	0.21	0.19	0.81	0.47	0.20	0.76
Portugal	0.10	0.07	0.78	0.09	0.02	0.61
Spain	0.52	0.38	3.51	0.47	0.57	3.69
Sweden	1.35	0.63	1.08	1.41	0.66	1.12
Switzerland	2.50	1.30	1.34	2.92	0.73	1.70
United Kingdom	4.38	1.27	1.78	6.97	1.49	3.25
China	0.10	2.21	0.78	0.57	3.02	0.79
India–Burma–Sri Lanka	2.71	1.02	1.39	1.23	0.46	1.05
Turkey	0.31	0.25	0.83	0.85	0.19	0.90
Egypt	1.04	0.33	1.00	0.85	0.44	0.90
Iran	0.00	0.00	0.76	0.00	0.00	0.58
Iraq	0.00	0.00	0.76	0.00	0.00	0.58
Libya	0.00	0.00	0.76	0.00	0.15	0.58
Argentina	1.25	0.49	1.05	0.85	0.00	0.90
Brazil	0.63	0.95	0.91	0.38	0.11	0.72
Bulgaria	0.42	3.04	0.86	0.85	3.10	0.90
Hungary	4.48	3.50	1.81	6.97	3.13	3.25
Poland	6.56	4.63	2.29	4.15	3.98	2.17
Romania	2.81	3.11	1.42	4.15	3.35	2.17
Soviet Union	1.04	45.58	10.20	1.32	43.14	14.28
Yugoslavia	2.40	2.38	1.32	4.43	2.88	2.28
Totals	96.04	88.13	96.53	96.32	86.84	95.59

Sources: Trade figures for 1928 are from League of Nations (1942). Figures for 1989 are
from International Monetary Fund (1990a).

TABLE A.5   **Hungary: geographical composition of trade by individual partner country, 1928, 1989, and predicted** (percentages of total)

Country	Imports			Exports		
	1928	1989	Predicted	1928	1989	Predicted
United States	3.63	1.60	2.78	0.82	2.83	2.77
Japan-Korea-Taiwan	0.00	1.47	5.10	0.00	1.24	1.80
Austria	16.20	6.87	4.29	34.02	5.36	12.99
Belgium-Luxembourg	0.84	1.67	2.74	0.82	0.83	1.75
Denmark	0.00	0.36	0.72	0.41	0.57	0.70
Finland	0.00	0.73	0.72	0.00	0.84	0.55
France	2.51	2.48	7.24	0.82	2.68	6.03
Germany	19.55	18.29	19.00	11.89	11.58	13.61
Greece	0.56	0.20	0.84	0.82	0.78	0.85
Italy	3.91	3.66	7.29	6.56	4.52	6.42
Netherlands	1.96	1.94	3.93	0.41	1.18	2.16
Norway	0.00	0.12	0.72	0.00	0.17	0.55
Portugal	0.00	0.07	0.72	0.00	0.03	0.55
Spain	0.28	0.36	3.27	0.41	0.49	3.49
Sweden	0.28	1.24	0.78	0.41	1.09	0.70
Switzerland	3.91	2.42	1.58	3.69	1.44	1.90
United Kingdom	2.79	1.90	1.33	2.87	1.50	1.60
China	0.00	0.85	0.72	0.00	1.12	0.55
India–Burma–Sri Lanka	1.40	0.74	1.03	0.41	0.58	0.70
Turkey	0.56	0.37	0.84	0.82	0.95	0.85
Egypt	0.28	0.17	0.78	0.41	0.42	0.70
Iran	0.00	0.05	0.72	0.00	0.86	0.55
Iraq	0.00	0.03	0.72	0.00	0.17	0.55
Libya	0.00	0.00	0.72	0.00	0.28	0.55
Argentina	0.28	0.06	0.78	0.00	0.03	0.55
Brazil	0.00	0.46	0.72	0.41	0.33	0.70
Bulgaria	0.84	1.20	0.90	0.82	1.05	0.85
Czechoslovakia	22.35	5.31	5.65	17.62	5.80	6.99
Poland	4.19	3.16	1.64	3.28	2.24	1.75
Romania	7.82	1.58	2.44	5.33	1.82	2.50
Soviet Union	0.28	24.28	14.94	0.41	28.29	18.01
Yugoslavia	5.03	3.00	1.83	6.56	3.51	2.95
Totals	99.44	86.63	97.47	100.00	84.58	97.14

Sources: Trade figures for 1928 are from League of Nations (1942). Figures for 1989 are from International Monetary Fund (1990a).

TABLE A.6   Poland: geographical composition of trade by individual
partner country, 1928, 1989, and predicted (percentages of
total)

Country	Imports			Exports		
	1928	1989	Predicted	1928	1989	Predicted
United States	13.95	1.78	5.43	0.84	2.73	2.94
Japan-Korea-Taiwan	0.00	1.41	5.47	0.42	0.97	2.06
Austria	6.58	4.46	2.33	12.39	3.20	5.37
Belgium-Luxembourg	2.04	1.34	3.22	2.31	1.50	2.42
Denmark	1.57	0.54	1.14	3.15	1.33	1.80
Finland	0.16	1.01	0.81	1.05	1.43	0.99
France	7.52	2.41	8.95	1.68	2.99	6.70
Germany	26.96	12.93	22.13	34.66	13.57	23.18
Greece	0.16	0.16	0.81	0.00	0.42	0.58
Italy	2.51	3.07	7.49	1.89	2.47	4.98
Netherlands	4.08	3.10	4.71	3.15	2.28	3.34
Norway	0.47	0.46	0.88	0.84	0.36	0.90
Portugal	0.00	0.02	0.77	0.00	0.05	0.58
Spain	0.16	0.31	3.47	0.21	0.40	3.61
Sweden	2.04	1.49	1.25	4.41	2.17	2.28
Switzerland	2.66	4.58	1.40	0.63	2.94	0.82
United Kingdom	9.40	3.85	3.00	8.82	5.43	3.99
China	0.16	2.49	0.81	0.42	2.69	0.74
India–Burma–Sri Lanka	3.29	1.06	1.55	0.00	0.55	0.58
Turkey	0.00	0.49	0.77	0.00	0.69	0.58
Egypt	0.47	0.03	0.88	0.21	0.32	0.66
Iran	0.00	0.40	0.77	0.00	0.33	0.58
Iraq	0.00	0.98	0.77	0.00	0.23	0.58
Libya	0.00	0.00	0.77	0.00	1.53	0.58
Argentina	1.25	0.17	1.07	0.21	0.09	0.66
Brazil	0.63	1.93	0.92	0.21	1.15	0.66
Bulgaria	0.16	1.65	0.81	0.00	2.01	0.58
Czechoslovakia	6.27	4.96	2.25	11.76	5.99	5.12
Hungary	1.25	2.13	1.07	1.68	2.21	1.23
Romania	1.10	1.49	1.03	2.10	1.34	1.39
Soviet Union	1.10	26.11	8.96	1.68	24.96	13.89
Yugoslavia	0.31	3.22	0.84	1.05	2.59	0.99
Totals	96.24	90.04	96.53	95.80	90.90	95.36

Sources: Trade figures for 1928 are from League of Nations (1942). Figures for 1989 are
from International Monetary Fund (1990a).

TABLE A.7   Romania: geographical composition of trade by individual
partner country, 1928, 1989, and predicted (percentages of
total)

Country	Imports			Exports		
	1928	1989	Predicted	1928	1989	Predicted
United States	5.44	1.60	3.31	0.37	2.47	2.73
Japan-Korea-Taiwan	0.00	0.51	5.31	0.00	1.39	1.88
Austria	11.48	0.40	3.38	11.36	0.43	4.92
Belgium-Luxembourg	2.72	0.27	3.28	1.47	0.32	2.08
Denmark	0.00	0.08	0.75	0.73	0.08	0.86
Finland	0.00	0.02	0.75	0.00	0.11	0.57
France	4.53	1.39	7.99	4.03	2.92	7.55
Germany	23.56	3.19	20.68	24.91	5.21	19.25
Greece	0.60	0.45	0.89	4.40	0.42	2.26
Italy	7.55	0.93	8.42	12.82	5.76	9.13
Netherlands	1.51	0.70	3.98	1.10	0.81	2.53
Norway	0.30	0.01	0.82	0.37	0.25	0.71
Portugal	0.00	0.03	0.75	0.00	0.04	0.57
Spain	0.30	0.07	3.40	0.73	0.77	3.78
Sweden	0.91	0.22	0.96	0.00	0.27	0.57
Switzerland	2.42	0.19	1.30	1.10	0.16	1.00
United Kingdom	9.37	0.64	2.90	3.66	1.23	1.98
China	0.00	2.72	0.75	0.00	2.66	0.57
India–Burma–Sri Lanka	0.60	1.73	0.89	0.00	1.17	0.57
Turkey	1.21	0.73	1.02	2.20	1.40	1.42
Egypt	1.51	3.17	1.09	4.40	2.33	2.26
Iran	0.00	7.65	0.75	0.00	2.34	0.57
Iraq	0.00	1.54	0.75	0.00	4.03	0.57
Libya	0.00	0.70	0.75	0.00	0.36	0.57
Argentina	0.00	0.09	0.75	0.37	0.13	0.71
Brazil	0.00	0.40	0.75	0.00	0.07	0.57
Bulgaria	0.91	4.88	0.96	1.47	2.41	1.14
Czechoslovakia	14.50	5.33	4.08	7.33	3.70	3.38
Hungary	4.53	1.91	1.79	9.52	1.01	4.22
Poland	4.23	1.79	1.72	2.20	1.05	1.42
Soviet Union	0.60	36.04	11.59	0.00	30.41	13.96
Yugoslavia	0.91	1.21	0.96	1.83	1.00	1.28
Totals	99.70	80.60	97.43	96.34	76.71	95.61

Sources: Trade figures for 1928 are from League of Nations (1942). Figures for 1989 are
from International Monetary Fund (1990a).

TABLE A.8 Soviet Union: geographical composition of trade by individual partner country, 1928, 1989, and predicted (percentages of total)

Country	Imports			Exports		
	1928	1989	Predicted	1928	1989	Predicted
United States	19.61	5.71	6.94	3.86	1.27	4.26
Japan-Korea-Taiwan	0.48	4.12	5.73	2.00	4.90	2.77
Austria	1.68	1.22	1.20	1.00	1.14	1.00
Belgium-Luxembourg	0.24	0.72	2.87	1.72	1.89	2.28
Denmark	0.24	0.34	0.85	1.29	0.39	1.12
Finland	1.56	4.53	1.17	0.72	4.44	0.89
France	3.76	2.30	8.26	5.44	4.23	8.47
Germany	25.03	8.22	22.23	24.46	7.21	19.97
Greece	0.00	0.19	0.79	0.57	0.41	0.83
Italy	1.08	3.45	7.34	3.29	5.81	5.73
Netherlands	0.36	0.90	3.93	2.29	2.13	3.12
Norway	0.48	0.23	0.91	0.29	0.40	0.72
Portugal	0.00	0.16	0.79	0.00	0.10	0.60
Spain	0.36	0.57	3.61	1.29	2.08	4.18
Sweden	1.81	0.50	1.23	0.29	1.28	0.72
Switzerland	0.12	0.80	0.82	0.00	0.39	0.60
United Kingdom	4.45	1.49	1.87	20.74	2.19	8.92
China	6.02	2.27	2.25	4.29	3.14	2.32
India–Burma–Sri Lanka	3.49	4.81	1.64	0.57	2.99	0.83
Turkey	1.44	0.38	1.14	1.86	0.79	1.35
Egypt	3.73	0.21	1.70	1.14	0.42	1.06
Iran	0.00	0.00	0.79	0.00	0.00	0.60
Iraq	0.00	0.00	0.79	0.00	0.00	0.60
Libya	0.00	0.00	0.79	0.00	0.06	0.60
Argentina	5.17	1.27	2.05	0.14	0.02	0.66
Brazil	0.36	0.41	0.88	0.00	0.07	0.60
Bulgaria	0.00	9.30	0.86	0.00	8.87	0.73
Czechoslovakia	2.17	9.94	2.02	0.57	9.41	2.85
Hungary	0.12	3.86	1.81	0.00	3.94	2.18
Poland	0.96	4.37	2.52	1.72	4.66	3.96
Romania	0.00	5.80	1.54	0.14	6.24	1.84
Yugoslavia	0.00	3.61	2.34	0.00	3.62	2.34
Totals	84.72	81.66	93.64	79.69	84.46	88.72

Sources: Trade figures for 1928 are from League of Nations (1942). Figures for 1989 are from International Monetary Fund (1990a).

TABLE A.9   Yugoslavia: geographical composition of trade by individual partner country, 1928, 1989, and predicted (percentages of total)

Country	Imports			Exports		
	1928	1989	Predicted	1928	1989	Predicted
United States	5.15	5.14	3.17	1.04	5.13	2.99
Japan-Korea-Taiwan	0.00	1.98	5.19	0.00	0.39	1.88
Austria	17.60	4.52	4.68	18.23	3.41	7.56
Belgium-Luxembourg	0.86	1.21	2.79	0.52	0.77	1.72
Denmark	0.00	0.47	0.73	0.00	0.24	0.58
Finland	0.00	0.18	0.73	0.00	0.54	0.58
France	4.72	4.47	7.86	4.17	3.74	7.61
Germany	13.73	17.64	18.02	11.98	12.34	14.31
Greece	1.29	0.71	1.02	8.33	1.59	3.77
Italy	12.02	10.62	9.24	26.04	15.41	14.21
Netherlands	0.86	1.99	3.75	0.52	1.38	2.31
Norway	0.00	0.21	0.73	0.00	0.30	0.58
Portugal	0.00	0.03	0.73	0.00	0.05	0.58
Spain	0.00	0.37	3.26	0.00	0.43	3.51
Sweden	0.43	1.34	0.83	0.00	1.58	0.58
Switzerland	1.29	2.01	1.02	3.13	1.92	1.77
United Kingdom	5.58	2.01	1.98	1.56	2.49	1.17
China	0.00	0.44	0.73	0.00	0.44	0.58
India–Burma–Sri Lanka	1.72	0.43	1.12	0.52	0.90	0.77
Turkey	0.43	0.65	0.83	0.00	1.32	0.58
Egypt	0.43	0.32	0.83	0.52	1.15	0.77
Iran	0.00	0.84	0.73	0.00	0.99	0.58
Iraq	0.00	2.80	0.73	0.00	2.24	0.58
Libya	0.00	1.48	0.73	0.00	0.50	0.58
Argentina	0.43	0.16	0.83	0.52	0.01	0.77
Brazil	2.58	1.13	1.31	0.00	0.04	0.58
Bulgaria	0.43	1.06	0.83	0.52	0.96	0.77
Czechoslovakia	18.03	3.31	4.78	8.85	2.97	3.97
Hungary	6.87	2.58	2.27	8.85	2.10	3.97
Poland	2.58	3.20	1.31	1.56	3.18	1.17
Romania	2.58	1.05	1.31	1.04	0.87	0.97
Soviet Union	0.00	15.13	13.40	0.00	19.85	13.87
Totals	99.57	89.48	97.46	97.92	89.22	96.21

Sources: Trade figures for 1928 are from League of Nations (1942). Figures for 1989 are from International Monetary Fund (1990a).

B Aggregate Demand Effects of Asymmetric Import Demand from EESU

In this appendix we complement the discussion in chapter 3 by presenting a more formal analysis of the aggregate demand effects of capital flows to EESU. For ease of exposition, we ignore regions other than the United States, the European Community, and EESU. The focus is on the differential macroeconomic impact when EESU import demand falls disproportionately on the European Community.

We treat import demand in EESU parametrically and call it Δ. We assume that $(1-\alpha)$ of that demand falls on the United States, and the rest on the European Community. To make our point as starkly as possible, we use the standard fix-price Keynesian model where output is demand determined (but see the remarks below). We express aggregate demand in the United States and the Community as follows:

(B.1) $$Y = A(Y, r) + B(Y, y) + (1 - \alpha)\, \Delta$$

(B.2) $$y = a(y, r) + b(y, Y) + \alpha\Delta$$

(B.3) $$B(Y, y) + b(y, Y) = 0.$$

where A is US absorption, r is the interest rate, which is common to both regions, and B is net exports of the United States to the European Community, so that $B + (1 - \alpha)\Delta$ is total US net exports. (The lowercase counterparts of A, B, and Y have the analogous interpretation for the Community). Equation (B.3) states that net exports have to net out when aggregated over all countries. The partial derivatives of absorption and net exports with respect to income and interest rates have the usual signs.

These three equations determine three endogenous variables (Y, y, and r) as functions of import demand from EESU (Δ). Since our focus is on the impact of the asymmetry arising from α, it is convenient to ignore all other sources of asymmetry. In particular, we assume that the United States and the Community are of identical size and that their economic structures are the same. This allows us to set $a_r = A_r$, $a_y = A_Y$, $b_y = B_Y$, and $b_Y = B_y$, where the subscripts indicate partial derivatives.

We can now solve for the effects of an increase in Δ by performing comparative static analysis on the system above. With respect to the interest rate we get:

(B.4) $dr/d\Delta = -\dfrac{1}{2} A_r > 0,$

which is the positive interest rate shock of the increased demand for capital in EESU. The effects on output in the United States and the European Community are:

(B.5) $dY/d\Delta = [(1 - 2\alpha)/2]\{1 - A_y + B_y - B_Y\}$

(B.6) $dy/d\Delta = -[(1 - 2\alpha)/2]\{1 - A_y + B_y - B_Y\}.$

Since $(1 - A_y) > 0$, $B_y > 0$, and $B_Y < 0$ under standard assumptions, the expression in braces in each of these equations is necessarily positive. We note that when the demand shock is symmetric ($\alpha = \frac{1}{2}$), aggregate demand and output remain unchanged in each of the two regions. Moreover, even when the shock is not symmetric, the aggregate demand effect for the two regions combined is zero, since the two expressions above are of identical magnitude and opposite sign.

However, when α is different from $\frac{1}{2}$, one of the two regions receives a boost in output and the other a decline. In particular, if $\alpha > \frac{1}{2}$, so that most of EESU import demand falls on the European Community, aggregate demand must fall in the United States and increase in the Community. It can also be checked that US net exports to the Community must rise as a result of the asymmetry.

The Keynesian model relies exclusively on changes in income as an equilibrating mechanism in response to the US–EC asymmetry. An adjustment in the value of the dollar can play a similar role. A dollar depreciation against the European currencies helps improve the US current account and takes the pressure off US aggregate demand. However, exchange rate flexibility is not an unqualified savior for the United States. Besides the possibility that the short-run aggregate demand effect of a dollar depreciation can go the wrong way, such a depreciation also reduces US real income by worsening the external terms of trade.

C Private-Sector Investment in Eastern Europe and the Soviet Union: Survey Results

This appendix describes the results of a mailed survey of firms in various industries on their existing investments and intentions regarding investment in Eastern Europe and the Soviet Union. The discussion below is based on the 54 responses that were returned (for some questions, only 53 responses were available). Of these firms, 33 percent identify themselves as primarily engaged in financial services, 30 percent in manufacturing consumer goods, and 6 percent in manufacturing machines or transport equipment. The sample is primarily composed of large (i.e., Fortune 500) firms. It includes firms based in Europe and Japan as well as in the United States.

We asked firms a number of questions about their existing investments in the region, including their type, magnitude, and location by country. We then asked similar questions about anticipated investments over the next five years. Finally, we asked firms about their perceptions of the importance of a variety of potential obstacles and attractions to investing in the region and of the current investment climate in each country.

Table C.1 describes the extent of existing and expected future involvement in the region. It shows that 61 percent of the firms responding had no investments in Eastern Europe, and that most of the existing investment is quite small—less than 1 percent of the firm's total foreign investment. Only 28 percent of the respondents expect to have no investments in Eastern Europe at the end of five years. (The percentage not responding rises from 5.6 percent to 9.4 percent, which we take as an indicator of increased uncertainty.) Again, most of the firms that expect to become involved in the region anticipate small investments. An additional 14 percent anticipate spending 1 percent or less of their total foreign investments in the region, 7.6 percent and 5.7 percent

TABLE C.1 **Extent of investment by Western firms in Eastern Europe and the Soviet Union** (percentages of total sample)

Percentage of total foreign investment	Eastern Europe		Soviet Union	
	Existing	Anticipated	Existing	Anticipated
None	61.1	28.3	70.4	41.5
1	31.5	45.3	24.1	30.2
2	0.0	5.7	0.0	7.5
3	0.0	1.9	0.0	1.9
4–6	0.0	5.7	0.0	3.8
6–10	0.0	1.9	1.9	3.8
>10	1.9	1.9	0.0	3.8
No response	5.6	9.4	3.7	7.5

Source: Private-sector survey conducted by the authors. See text for survey methodology.

anticipate spending 2 percent to 3 percent and 4 percent to 6 percent, respectively, of total foreign investment in the region.

Fewer of the respondents have existing investments in the Soviet Union. Seventy percent have no existing investments, but just 41 percent expect to have no investment in five years—again a drop of roughly 30 percentage points. Although the anticipated investments are a little larger than for Eastern Europe, overall the magnitudes are still quite small.

What form do these investments take? Table C.2 shows that the most common type of existing investment is a branch or office. This is followed by joint ventures and subsidiaries. Not surprisingly, relatively few firms have licensing agreements, portfolio investments, or franchises in the region. However, joint ventures and subsidiaries are expected to become as common as branches or offices over the next five years. All types of investment are expected to increase.

We look next at existing and anticipated investment by country. Table C.3 shows the percentage of firms in our sample that are currently or expect to be investors in each country. Not surprisingly, the countries with the largest percentages of firms as current investors are Hungary

TABLE C.2   **Investment by Western firms in Eastern Europe and the Soviet Union, by type** (percentages of total sample)

Type	Existing	Anticipated
Branch or office	50.0	43.3
Joint venture	22.2	49.1
Subsidiary	18.5	41.5
Licensing agreement	14.8	17.0
Portfolio investment[a]	9.3	15.1
Franchise	1.9	5.7

a. Includes loans.

Source: Private-sector survey conducted by the authors. See text for survey methodology.

and the Soviet Union (with 44 percent and 41 percent of the respondents). The former East Germany follows as a distant third—26 percent of the firms have existing investments there—followed by Czechoslovakia with 22 percent and Poland with 20 percent.

If firms actually carry out their anticipated investments over the next five years, all of these countries will enjoy substantial increases in the number of firms investing within their borders. (However, the percentage of the sample that did not respond to these questions also rises, which we interpret as reflecting uncertainty about investment plans.) Hungary and the Soviet Union will continue to attract investments from the largest number of private firms (57 percent and 53 percent, respectively). Czechoslovakia will be a close third, receiving investments from more than half of the firms in our sample, followed by Poland. The number of firms investing in both countries is more than twice the number of current investors. About 13 percent of the firms anticipate investing in Bulgaria and Romania, with slightly more planning to invest in Yugoslavia—the country that appears to raise the greatest uncertainties.

Table C.3 suggests that there will be substantial increases in the number of firms that invest in Eastern Europe and in the Soviet Union. How large are these investments likely to be? It is difficult to estimate

TABLE C.3 Investment by Western firms in Eastern Europe and the Soviet Union, by host country (percentages of total sample)

Country	Existing investments			Anticipated investments		
	No investment	Some investment	No response	No investment	Some investment	No response
Bulgaria	81.5	12.9	5.6	77.4	13.2	9.4
Czechoslovakia	72.2	22.2	5.6	39.6	51.0	9.4
Former East Germany	68.5	25.9	5.6	60.4	30.2	9.4
Hungary	50.0	44.4	5.6	35.8	56.7	7.5
Poland	74.1	20.3	5.6	47.2	43.4	9.4
Romania	85.2	9.2	5.6	77.4	13.2	9.7
Soviet Union	55.6	40.7	3.7	39.6	52.9	7.5
Yugoslavia	77.8	14.8	7.4	69.8	17.0	13.2

Source: Private-sector survey conducted by the authors. See text for survey methodology.

TABLE C.4 Average value of investment by Western firms in Eastern Europe and the Soviet Union, by host country (thousands of dollars)[a]

Country	Existing	Anticipated	Ratio of anticipated to existing
Bulgaria	111.8	740.1	6.6
Czechoslovakia	1,631.9	5,213.5	3.2
Former East Germany	3,101.0	5,262.0	1.7
Hungary	4,123.5	6,688.3	1.6
Poland	172.5	4,192.7	24.3
Romania	23.0	221.9	9.6
Soviet Union	3,604.3	9,052.0	2.5
Yugoslavia	1,065.0	1,380.4	1.3

a. Respondents were asked whether their existing and anticipated investments in each country were none (coded as 0), less than $50,000 (1), between $50,000 and $100,000 (2), between $100,000 and $1 million (3), between $1 million and $5 million (4), or greater than $5 million (5). The results reported above are weighted averages of their responses, coded as follows: 0: none; 1: $25,000; 2: $75,000; 3: $500,000; 4: $2.5 million; and 5: $25 million.

Source: Private-sector survey conducted by the authors. See text for methodology.

an aggregate flow to each country from our sample, since it does not provide any information about the total number of private firms that may be involved.

Table C.4 provides an index of average investment by country, constructed to overstate anticipated levels. (Details are provided in the notes to the table.) It shows that by far the largest increase in average investment magnitudes is expected in Poland. Average investment is expected to triple in the Soviet Union, to more than double in Czechoslovakia, and to rise by 60 percent to 70 percent in Hungary and the former East Germany. Still, because of the overall base, the average value of investments in the sample remains quite small. In Poland for example, only 15 percent of firms anticipate making investments of more than $5 million. Only 17 percent of firms plan to invest more than

TABLE   C.5   Investment by Western firms in Eastern Europe and the
Soviet Union as a share of their total foreign investment
(percentages)[a]

	Existing	Anticipated	Ratio of anticipated to existing
Eastern Europe	0.627	1.479	2.4
Soviet Union	0.403	1.693	4.2

a. Respondents were asked whether their existing and anticipated investments in each country were none (coded as 0), 1 percent (1), 2 percent (2), 3 percent (3), 4 percent to 6 percent (4), 6 percent to 10 percent (5), or greater than 10 percent (6). The values reported above are weighted averages of their responses, coded as follows: 0: none; 1: 1 percent; 2: 2 percent; 3: 3 percent; 4: 5 percent; 5: 8 percent; and 6: 15 percent.

Source: Private-sector survey conducted by the authors. See text for survey methodology.

$5 million in Czechoslovakia, and 23 percent plan to invest more than $5 million in Hungary.

Table C.5 shows actual and anticipated investment as a percentage of total foreign investment of each firm—another measure of investment magnitudes. On average, just 0.6 percent of past foreign investments have gone to Eastern Europe and 0.4 percent to the Soviet Union. These figures are anticipated to rise to 1.5 percent and 1.7 percent of foreign investment, respectively. These figures suggest that private investment in Eastern Europe overall can be expected to more than double over the next five years, while private investment in the Soviet Union can be expected to quadruple.

Table C.6 shows firms' perceptions of the overall investment climate in each country. The first column in the table reports an index that ranges from 1 = very poor to 5 = excellent. Hungary and the former East Germany receive slightly positive ratings and are the only countries that received some rankings of 5. Czechoslovakia receives a neutral rating, whereas Poland overall receives a slightly negative rating, with just 15 percent of firms awarding it a 4. (Interestingly, the investment climate ratings are somewhat divorced from the extent of liberalization that has actually been undertaken. Poland, which has moved most

TABLE C.6   Assessment by Western firms of overall investment climate in
Eastern Europe and the Soviet Union, by country

Country	Average of responses[a]	Percentage of respondents giving positive rating[b]
Bulgaria	1.34	0.0
Czechoslovakia	2.96	26.0
Former East Germany	3.49	55.3
Hungary	3.24	46.0
Poland	2.68	18.0
Romania	1.26	0.0
Soviet Union	2.16	10.0
Yugoslavia	2.08	8.0

a. Respondents were asked to rate the investment climate in each country on a scale of
1 to 5, with 1 = very poor and 5 = excellent.

b. Defined as a response of either 4 or 5 on the above scale.

Source: Private-sector survey conducted by the authors. See text for survey methodology.

quickly, receives a negative rating whereas Hungary, which has not, is
rated positively.) The investment climate in Yugoslavia is ranked below
that in the Soviet Union—but substantially above that in either Bulgaria
or Romania.

Finally, we look at various factors that contribute to firms' assessments of investment opportunities in the region. Table C.7 shows how
firms on average ranked nine possible obstacles to investment. The
scale of this index ranges from 1 = not significant to 5 = strong
deterrent. "Political uncertainty" appears at the top of the list, with an
index close to 4. Three other obstacles—"uncertainty about economic
policies," "inability to repatriate earnings and/or capital gains," and
"lack of legal protection for private property"—receive nearly identical
ratings. Firms are somewhat less concerned about "poor distribution
systems" and "bureaucratic requirements" and only somewhat concerned about the productivity of the labor force. Overall, these views
are not surprising.

TABLE C.7 Perceived obstacles to investment in Eastern Europe and the
Soviet Union

Obstacle	Average of responses
Political uncertainty	3.98
Uncertainty about economic policies	3.90
Lack of legal protection for private property	3.83
Inability to repatriate earnings and/or capital gains	3.81
Poor economic prospects of the countries	3.69
Bureaucratic requirements	3.38
Poor distribution system	3.23
Lack of information	3.20
Inadequately trained or unproductive workers	2.83

a. Respondents were asked to rate each item on a scale of 1 to 5, with 1 = not significant and 5 = strong deterrent.

Source: Private-sector survey conducted by the authors. See text for survey methodology.

Table C.8 shows which factors firms view as major attractions to investing in the region. This index ranges from 1 = not significant to 5 = strong attraction. Here we did find some surprises. First, the greatest attractions to investing are "new and expanding markets" within the region and the "potential to beat out competitors by being first." Unless there are large transportation costs or trade barriers, growing markets are not a reason for investing in a new market per se—they are typically a reason for increasing exports. The second surprise was that firms do not view low labor costs and the presence of skilled workers as strong attractions. These of course would provide strong economic reasons for investing in the area.

It is interesting that over half of the firms claim that they expect their competitors to increase their investments (giving this factor either a 4 or a 5) in Eastern Europe or the Soviet Union. Although this may explain why so many firms believe it is important to beat out their competitors, this ranking seems to imply a much greater increase in private investment than our results suggest is likely. In other words,

TABLE C.8   Perceived attractions to investment in Eastern Europe and the Soviet Union

Attraction	Average of responses
New and expanding market	3.96
Potential to beat out competitors by being first	3.15
Proximity to EC markets	2.84
Low labor costs	2.64
Skilled labor forces	2.51
Investment incentives by Western or host governments	2.19
Political or other ties to the region	1.87

a. Respondents were asked to rate each item on a scale of 1 to 5, with 1 = not significant to 5 = strong attraction.

Source: Private-sector survey conducted by the authors. See text for survey methodology.

firms appear to anticipate modest to moderate increases in their own investment, but to expect that their competitors are going to expand investments in the region strongly. Alternatively, they view their own plans as reflecting a rapid increase in investment also—which still translates into small magnitudes given the low initial base.

References

Alexander, Lewis, and Joseph Gagnon. 1990. "The Global Economic Implications of German Unification." *International Finance Discussion Paper* no. 379. Washington: Board of Governors of the Federal Reserve System.

Blanchard, Olivier, and Richard Layard. 1990. "Economic Change in Poland." *CEPR Discussion Paper* no. 432. London: Centre for Economic Policy Research.

Brabant, Josef M. van. 1989. *Economic Integration in Eastern Europe—A Handbook.* New York: Routledge.

Burda, Michael. 1990. "The Consequences of German Monetary and Economic Union." *CEPR Discussion Paper* no. 449. London: Centre for Economic Policy Research.

Central Intelligence Agency. 1989. *Handbook of Economic Statistics.* Washington: Government Printing Office.

Central Intelligence Agency. 1990a. *Handbook of Economic Statistics.* Washington: Government Printing Office.

Central Intelligence Agency. 1990b. "Eastern Europe: Long Road Ahead to Economic Well-Being." Paper presented to the Joint Economic Committee of Congress (May).

Centre for Economic Policy Research. 1990. *Monitoring European Integration—The Impact of Eastern Europe.* London: Centre for Economic Policy Research (October).

Cohen, Daniel. 1990. "Slow Growth and Large LDC Debt in the Eighties: An Update." Paris: CEPREMAP.

Commission of the European Communities. 1990. "Stabilization, Liberalization and Devolution: Assessment of the Economic Reform Process in the Soviet Union." *European Economy* no. 45. Brussels: Commission of the European Communities (December).

Congressional Budget Office. 1990. *How the Economic Transformations in Europe Will Affect the United States.* Washington: Government Printing Office (December).

Deutsche Bank Economics Department. 1990. "Unification Issues: The Costs of German Unification and Ways to Finance Them." Frankfurt: Deutsche Bank (mimeographed, November).

Diwan, Ishac. 1990. "The Effect of Changes in Eastern Europe on the World Financial Markets." Washington: World Bank (mimeographed).

Economic Commission for Europe. 1990. *Economic Survey of Europe in 1989–1990.* Geneva: United Nations.

Fieleke, Norman. 1990. "Commerce with the Newly Liberalizing Countries: Promised Land, Quicksand, or What?" *New England Economic Review* (May/June).

Genberg, Hans. 1990. "On the Sequencing of Reforms in Eastern Europe." Geneva: Graduate Institute of International Studies.

Giustiniani, A., F. Papadia, and D. Porciani. 1991. "The Effects of the Eastern European Countries' Economic Reform on the Western Industrial Economies: A Macroeconomic Approach." Rome: Bank of Italy (mimeographed).

Hansson, Ardo. 1990. "The 1948 West German Economic Reforms: A Model for Eastern Europe?" *University of British Columbia Department of Economics Discussion Paper* no. 90-05. Vancouver: University of British Columbia.

Hinds, Manuel. 1990. "Issues in the Introduction of Market Forces in Eastern European Socialist Economies." Washington: World Bank (April).

Hirschman, Albert O. 1990. "Good News Is Not Bad News." *New York Review of Books* (11 October).

International Monetary Fund. 1989. *World Economic Outlook.* Washington: International Monetary Fund.

International Monetary Fund. 1990a. *International Financial Statistics.* Washington: International Monetary Fund (October).

International Monetary Fund. 1990b. *World Economic Outlook.* Washington: International Monetary Fund.

IMF et al. 1990. *The Economy of the USSR* (the Houston Summit Report). Washington: World Bank.

Kenen, Peter B. 1991. "Transitional Arrangements for Trade and Payments Among the CMEA Countries." *IMF Staff Papers.* Washington: International Monetary Fund (forthcoming, September).

Kornai, Janos. 1990. *The Road to a Free Economy—Shifting from a Socialist System: The Example of Hungary.* New York: W.W. Norton.

Kostrzewa, Wojciech, Peter Nunenkamp, and Holger Schmieding. 1989. "Marshall Plan for Middle and Eastern Europe?" *Working Paper* no. 403. Kiel: Kiel Institute of World Economics.

League of Nations. 1942. *The Network of World Trade.* Geneva: League of Nations.

Lipton, David, and Jeffrey Sachs. 1990. "Creating a Market Economy in Eastern Europe: The Case of Poland." *Brookings Papers on Economic Activity* 1:75–133.

Organization for Economic Cooperation and Development. 1991. "The International Trade and Financial Situation of Eastern Europe in 1989–90." *Financial Market Trends* no. 45. Paris: Organization for Economic Cooperation and Development (February).

Portes, Richard. 1990. "The Transition to Convertibility for Eastern Europe and the USSR." *CEPR Discussion Paper* no. 500. London: Centre for Economic Policy Research.

Schrenk, Martin. 1990. "The CMEA System of Trade and Payments: Today and Tomorrow," *Strategic Planning and Review Discussion Paper* no. 5. Washington: World Bank (January).

Summers, Robert, and Alan Heston. 1988. "A New Set of International Comparisons of Real Product and Price Levels: Estimates for 130 Countries." *Review of Income and Wealth* 34: 1–25.

United Nations. 1987. *Industrial Statistics Yearbook.* New York: United Nations.

Wallich, Henry. 1955. *Mainsprings of the German Revival.* New Haven: Yale University Press.

Williamson, John. 1991. *The Economic Opening of Eastern Europe.* POLICY ANALYSES IN INTERNATIONAL ECONOMICS 31. Washington: Institute for International Economics.

World Bank. 1990a. *World Development Indicators.* Washington: World Bank.

World Bank. 1990b. *World Development Report.* Washington: World Bank.

Other Publications From the Institute

POLICY ANALYSES IN INTERNATIONAL ECONOMICS

32   Eastern Europe and the Soviet Union in the World Economy
Susan M. Collins and Dani Rodrik/*May 1991*
$12.95   ISBN 0-88132-157-5   172 pp

BOOKS

IMF Conditionality
John Williamson, editor/*1983*
$35.00 (cloth only)   ISBN 0-88132-006-4   695 pp

Trade Policy in the 1980s
William R. Cline, editor/*1983*
$35.00 (cloth)   ISBN 0-88132-008-1   810 pp
$20.00 (paper)   ISBN 0-88132-031-5   810 pp

Subsidies in International Trade
Gary Clyde Hufbauer and Joanna Shelton Erb/*1984*
$35.00 (cloth only)   ISBN 0-88132-004-8   299 pp

International Debt: Systemic Risk and Policy Response
William R. Cline/*1984*
$30.00 (cloth only)   ISBN 0-88132-015-3   336 pp

Trade Protection in the United States: 31 Case Studies
Gary Clyde Hufbauer, Diane E. Berliner, and Kimberly Ann Elliott/*1986*
$25.00   ISBN 0-88132-040-4   371 pp

Toward Renewed Economic Growth in Latin America
Bela Balassa, Gerardo M. Bueno, Pedro-Pablo Kuczynski, and
   Mario Henrique Simonsen/*1986*
$15.00   ISBN 0-88132-045-5   205 pp

American Trade Politics: System Under Stress
I. M. Destler/*1986*
$30.00 (cloth)   ISBN 0-88132-058-7   380 pp
$18.00 (paper)   ISBN 0-88132-057-9   380 pp

The Future of World Trade in Textiles and Apparel
William R. Cline/*1987, rev. June 1990*
$20.00   ISBN 0-88132-110-9   344 pp

Capital Flight and Third World Debt
Donald R. Lessard and John Williamson, editors/*1987*
$16.00   ISBN 0-88132-053-6   270 pp

The Canada-United States Free Trade Agreement: The Global Impact
Jeffrey J. Schott and Murray G. Smith, editors/*1988*
$13.95   ISBN 0-88132-073-0   211 pp

Managing the Dollar: From the Plaza to the Louvre
Yoichi Funabashi/*1988, rev. 1989*
$19.95   ISBN 0-88132-097-8   307 pp

World Agricultural Trade: Building a Consensus
William M. Miner and Dale E. Hathaway, editors/*1988*
$16.95   ISBN 0-88132-071-3   226 pp

Japan in the World Economy
Bela Balassa and Marcus Noland/*1988*
$19.95   ISBN 0-88132-041-2   306 pp

America in the World Economy: A Strategy for the 1990s
C. Fred Bergsten/*1988*
$29.95 (cloth)   ISBN 0-88132-089-7   235 pp
$13.95 (paper)   ISBN 0-88132-082-X   235 pp

United States External Adjustment and the World Economy
William R. Cline/*May 1989*
$25.00   ISBN 0-88132-048-X   392 pp

Free Trade Areas and U.S. Trade Policy
Jeffrey J. Schott, editor/*May 1989*
$19.95   ISBN 0-88132-094-3   400 pp

Dollar Politics: Exchange Rate Policymaking in the United States
I. M. Destler and C. Randall Henning/*September 1989*
$11.95   ISBN 0-88132-079-X   192 pp

Foreign Direct Investment in the United States
Edward M. Graham and Paul R. Krugman/*December 1989*
$11.95   ISBN 0-88132-074-9   161 pp

Latin American Adjustment: How Much Has Happened?
John Williamson, editor/*April 1990*
$34.95   ISBN 0-88132-125-7   480 pp

Completing the Uruguay Round: A Results-Oriented
  Approach to the GATT Trade Negotiations/*September 1990*
Jeffrey J. Schott, editor
$19.95   ISBN 0-88132-130-3   256 pp

Economic Sanctions Reconsidered (in two volumes)
  History and Current Policy (also sold separately, see below)
  Supplemental Case Histories
Gary Clyde Hufbauer, Jeffrey J. Schott, and Kimberly Ann Elliott/
1985, 2d ed. December 1990
$65.00 (cloth)   ISBN 0-88132-015-X   928 pp
$45.00 (paper)   ISBN 0-88132-105-2   928 pp

Economic Sanctions Reconsidered: History and Current Policy
Gary Clyde Hufbauer, Jeffrey J. Schott, and Kimberly Ann Elliott/
2d ed. December 1990
$36.00 (cloth)   ISBN 0-88132-136-2   288 pp
$25.00 (paper)   ISBN 0-88132-140-0   288 pp

Pacific Basin Developing Countries: Prospects for the Future
Marcus Noland/*January 1991*
$29.95 (cloth)   ISBN 0-88132-141-9   250 pp
$19.95 (paper)   ISBN 0-88132-081-1   250 pp

SPECIAL REPORTS

1 **Promoting World Recovery: A Statement on Global**
   Economic Strategy
   by Twenty-six Economists from Fourteen Countries/*December 1982*
   (Out of print)   ISBN 0-88132-013-7   45 pp

2 **Prospects for Adjustment in Argentina, Brazil, and Mexico:**
   Responding to the Debt Crisis
   John Williamson, editor/*June 1983*
   (Out of print)   ISBN 0-88132-016-1   71 pp

3 **Inflation and Indexation: Argentina, Brazil, and Israel**
   John Williamson, editor/*March 1985*
   (Out of print)   ISBN 0-88132-037-4   191 pp

4 **Global Economic Imbalances**
   C. Fred Bergsten, editor/*March 1986*
   $25.00 (cloth)   ISBN 0-88132-038-2   126 pp
   $10.00 (paper)   ISBN 0-88132-042-0   126 pp

9079 ==

FORTHCOMING